Group Guidance and Counselling

Group Guidance and Counselling

Dr. Ramesh Chaturvedi

CRESCENT
PUBLISHING CORPORATION

[The responsibility for the facts stated, conclusions reached and plagiarism, if any, in this book is entirely that of the Author. And the Publisher bears no responsibility for them, whatsoever.]

Group Guidance and Counselling

First Published : 2013

ISBN 81-8342-073-7

Published by :

CRESCENT PUBLISHING CORPORATION
4831/24, Prahlad Street,
Ansari Road, Darya Ganj,
New Delhi - 110002
Ph. : 23272541, 23257835
Fax : 91- 011- 23257835
e-mail : campusbooks@hotmail.com

Printed at :
Roshan Offset Printers
Delhi

Preface

There is a natural tendency for people to gather in groups for mutually beneficial purposes. Through groups, individuals accomplish goals and relate to others in innovative and productive ways. People would not survive, let alone thrive, without involvement in groups. This reliance and interdependence is seen in all types of groups from those that are primarily task-oriented to those that are basically therapeutic. In order to be effective, group leaders must be aware of the power and potency of groups. They must plan ahead and they must be sensitive to the stage of development of the group.

Group counselling involves individuals who are having difficulties they wish to resolve that are of a personal, educational, social, or vocational nature. These groups are primarily run in educational institutions or agencies. They deal with specific, nonpathological problems that members are aware of prior to joining and which do not involve major personality changes. Counselling groups run best when the rules governing them are few and clear. If there are more than a dozen rules, many members will tend to forget some of them. Likewise, if the rules are vague, some members will inevitably violate the letter or spirit of them. In counselling groups, rules should follow the ethical standards of professional organisation. Members should agree to keep each others' confidentiality, not attack each other verbally or physically, to actively participate in the group process, and to speak one at a time.

Conducting effective group counselling relies on the preparation of group leaders and their abilities to plan and conduct groups. Extra time in preparation is crucial to the life of the group. This process includes screening of members, selecting a manageable number of group participants, establishing a regular place and time for the conducting of the group, and setting rules. In running groups leaders must then recognise and utilise group stages and employ appropriate counselling skills in a timely fashion. Successful group counselling is dependent on many factors. Ultimately, the secrets of conducting effective counselling groups are in learning how groups operate and then personally investing in them.

This book is an up-to-date and accessible guide to the principles and practice of working with small groups. It opens up new opportunities to apply proven guidance and counselling methods in small group settings. It is strongly recommended for counsellors, social workers and clinical psychologists seeking to treat anxiety and depression in a more cost-effective way.

Dr. Ramesh Chaturvedi

Contents

1

Group Counselling

A counselling group consists of between five and eight people, supported by a facilitator. Members meet together regularly to learn more about themselves and how they relate to others. Group counselling is an invaluable tool for self-learning and experimenting with different ways of behaving.

Goals of Group Counselling

— To give you the strength to be more open and assertive.

— To help you feel clearer about yourself as an individual.

— To develop your emotional awareness.

— To enable you to feel stronger and more confident.

Benefits of Group Counselling

The group is a place where you can experiment with different ways of behaving. You may want to try talking more, or being quieter than usual. You may find yourself disagreeing with people in the group on certain points and feel your opinions become more clearly defined. As you listen to other people's experiences, you will have a chance to compare them with your own. You will probably find that conversations you take part in during the group will help to enrich your friendships outside.

Impact Therapy and Group Counselling

Impact Therapy is a concrete approach to group leading with much emphasis on the leader leading the group. A number of different models of group counselling exist that tend to put much of the responsibility for the outcome of the group on the members rather than the leader. The emphasis of these models has been on the interpersonal dynamics or group process rather than on the intrapersonal experience of each individual.

The Impact Therapy approach to group leading puts more emphasis on the individual's needs and how the leader can make the group experience valuable for each member. Impact Therapy is an active, multi-sensory approach to counselling that encourages the leader to be creative by using props, chairs, movement, writing and drawing to tap into members' different learning styles. Impact Therapy integrates creative counselling techniques and ideas from RET, TA, Gestalt Therapy, Reality Therapy, Adlerian Therapy.

Core Beliefs of Impact Therapy

Impact Therapy stresses listening, thinking, action, and impact, whereas many other approaches primarily emphasise listening and facilitating. Impact Therapy group leaders are guided by the following four core beliefs:

1. People don't mind being led when they are led well.
2. Group counselling should be clear and concrete.
3. Group counselling should never be boring.
4. The leader is primarily responsible for what happens in a group session.

PPFF Map

The impact therapist uses the initials PPFF (purpose, plan, focus, funnel) as the primary organising "map" for setting up and conducting a group session.

Purpose. The leader is very clear as to the kind of group (educational, support, counselling, or therapy) and why the group is meeting.

Plan. The impact therapist always plans the session. Good planning of the warm-up, middle, and closing phases is essential and yet many leaders do not plan or plan superficially. In-depth planning helps greatly in making group sessions productive.

Focus. The Impact Therapy group leader consciously focuses the session; that is, sees to it that relevant topics or issues are discussed. One of the biggest problems in groups is that the session never focuses long enough for there to be impact. Without focus, members go from topic to topic, causing the interaction to be superficial or disjointed. Unfortunately many leaders have been trained to wait for the members to focus the session.

Funnel. The impact therapist is always thinking of how to funnel the session; that is, how to take the session to a deeper, more meaningful level. Impact Therapy leaders feel that it is their responsibility to funnel the session. Funnelling is accomplished by asking good thought-provoking questions, by using deepening exercises, or by working with an individual using theory and the other members. Sessions have much more impact when they are funnelled and often sessions will not funnel unless the leader actively intervenes and directs the group. The impact therapist believes that funnelling is the key to a successful group.

Courage and permission

The Impact Therapy group leader has the courage and permission to do what it takes to make a session productive. The leader is willing to take the session to a meaningful level by using counselling theory, psychodrama, the other members, or him or herself in whatever way that may have impact on the members. The leader is willing to draw out and cut off members when it is appropriate to do so. In order to focus and funnel a session, the leader often will need to interrupt and redirect the flow of conversation. Cutting off is an essential skill for group leading. Leaders who allow members to be inappropriate, ramble, distract the group, or tell long, detailed stories are not being as effective as they can be.

Creative activities

Using creative activities is an integral part of being an Impact Therapy group leader. The creative techniques help make the group session more engaging, interesting, and meaningful. The following are the creative techniques that have been useful in groups.

Large Newsprint Pad or Wipeboard. Many people are visual learners. The benefit of having something large to write on cannot be over emphasised. It is helpful to visually represent concepts or ideas to the group such as irrational and rational self-talk, lists generated by the members, time lines, TA drawings, or drawings of enmeshment.

Use of Movement. The Impact Therapy group leader often has members stand up and move around to make points more concrete or to generate energy in the group. Group exercises that involve movement are valuable (not dance or yoga, but simply moving according to some instruction). Having members "sculpt" how they feel about the group or move along a "progress" line as to how much they have progressed, or move along value continuums are excellent movement exercises. Having members move between chairs that represent different people, ego states, or goals can serve as a valuable visual and experiential learning activity. Physical movement can be very beneficial in groups.

Small Child's Chair. Another essential tool for Impact Therapy group leaders is a small child's chair which can be used in a variety of ways. The chair can be used to represent the Child ego state or the little boy or girl in each of the members. So often, when a member is struggling with an issue, part of the problem has to do with the child part of themselves. The small chair makes the struggle more concrete for members. Having members sit in the chair or even look at the chair can be quite impactful.

Shield. The impact therapist often will use a prop (some tangible item such as a shield, cup, filter, rubber band, or blocks) for an exercise or when working with an individual member. Frequently members talk about needing to shield themselves from verbal abuse from someone in their lives such as a parent, spouse, or boss. By having them hold a shield as they discuss how they need to protect themselves, the members get the point about how they can make themselves safe.

Other Props. Styrofoam cups are used to represent one's self-worth. Punching holes in the cup to indicate "leaks in self-esteem" or smashing the cup to represent how members allow themselves to be psychologically smashed are two ways that cups can be used. A furnace filter is a good prop for getting members to discuss how they may need to filter input from certain people in their lives. Rubber bands can be used regarding stress--each person can stretch the rubber band to the level of stress they are feeling and then discuss either adding to the stress or reducing the stress. Wooden blocks with holes in them and pegs that either fit in the holes or nearly fit, or definitely do not fit can be used to symbolise the "fit" of relationships in members' lives.

These are just some of the props that are used by the impact therapist to focus and funnel the session. The impact therapist believes that visual metaphors often are more effective than just verbal metaphors because the visual metaphor is more concrete.

Understanding Group Work

Many counsellors in the field included group counselling in their helping repertoire but, also, other forms of group work heretofore unsystematically addressed in counselling curricula: counsellors led committees and task forces, they conducted skill training groups, they facilitated education and prevention groups, and they sometimes worked with disturbed clientele in groups. In fact, the scope of group work practice exceeded the extent of the training in groups that was being provided by counsellor education programs.

The standards define group work as: a broad professional practice that refers to the giving of help or the accomplishment of tasks in a group setting. It involves the application of group theory and process by a capable professional practitioner to assist an interdependent collection of people to reach their mutual goals, which may be personal, interpersonal, or task-related in nature.

Key elements of this definition are that group work is a broad professional practice oriented to help-giving or to task-accomplishment. That is, group work is comprehensive, not restricted to any one particular methodology, such as group counselling or group therapy. Moreover, group work can be used to help people to grow and change, goals that are well within the heritage of group counselling, and to help people to solve task and work problems. These concepts give rise to the evolution underway to make group work training more consistent with the growing intensity and diversity of demands for group work practice.

According to the standards, four major types of group work are available for use:

(a) task/work group work;

(b) guidance/psychoeducation group work;

(c) counselling/interpersonal problem-solving group work; and

(d) psychotherapy/personality reconstruction group work. Each of these types is described briefly next, using their working title.

Task group work. The practitioner focuses on applying group dynamics principles and processes to facilitate the accomplishment of identified work goals in such groups as committees, task forces, teams, community organisations, and discussion groups.

Psychoeducation group work. The practitioner focuses on educating, preventing, and developing competencies in members through such structured groups as social skills, parenting, substance abuse, and life skills training.

Counselling group work. The practitioner focuses on helping group participants to resolve usually non-severe career, educational, personal, social, and developmental concerns through processes of interpersonal interaction, support, and problem-solving.

Psychotherapy group work. The practitioner seeks to help individual group members to understand and remediate their significant emotional and psychologicial problems, focusing on intrapersonal and interpersonal dynamics.

Of course, in reality considerable overlap may be found among these four types of group work. Psychotherapy group work may involve some educating and use of structure, as found typically in psychoeducational group work, for instance. Yet, the four group work types are helpful in conceptually marking the breadth of possible group work practice, in designing appropriate training for each, and in guiding valid application. Regardless of which group work type is being used, the practitioner needs to possess both a general and a unique set of competencies. Core skills that all group workers need to master are touched on here.

Core Skills in Group Work

All counsellors doing group work need to be able to do at least the following:

1. Encourage participation of group members.
2. Observe and identify group process events.

3. Attend to and acknowledge group member behaviour.
4. Clarify and summarise group member statements.
5. Open and close group sessions.
6. Impart information in the group when necessary.
7. Model effective group leader behaviour.
8. Engage in appropriate self-disclosure in the group.
9. Give and receive feedback in the group.
10. Ask open-ended questions in the group.
11. Empathise with group members.
12. Confront group members' behaviour.
13. Help group members attribute meaning to their experience.
14. Help group members to integrate and apply learnings.
15. Keep the group on task in accomplishing its goals.

These competencies represent the foundation for all group work practice. Counsellors who lead any of the four types of group work need to master additional competencies and obtain appropriate supervised experience, as indicated in the standards.

Relevant directions for group work practitioners

To be an effective and relevant group worker in today's world, a counsellor needs to first develop basic knowledge and skills in group work. Most counsellor education programs should be providing this training as a matter of course. In addition, specialising in a certain type of group work, such as group counselling or psychoeducation group leadership, requires the practitioner to obtain training and supervision that build upon the core competencies.

Many counsellor education programs are able to provide such training presently, or are gearing up to do so. However, it also is important for the counselling practitioner who is interested in group work to seek additional training and supervision through appropriate continuing education services, such as group work offerings sponsored by the American Counselling Association or the Association for Specialists in Group Work.

Group Counselling for Students with Disabilities

Students with disabilities are now being educated with same age peers under a model of education known as inclusion. Other models of special education assign students with disabilities to segregated classes for primary instruction by teachers with different training and certification. Only limited time, if any, is spent in the regular classroom. With inclusion, any academic services needed for students with disabilities are provided in the regular classroom. Services may include special materials or equipment, adapted lessons, or classroom aides.

The inclusion model hopes to bring about favourable academic and social benefits for students with and without disabilities. However, when students who were previously excluded from the classroom are now included, there are implications for the social structure within the class. Parents and teachers have been concerned that it will be difficult to integrate students with disabilities into the regular classroom. When school personnel utilise what is known about how groups form, work and process activities, then the inclusion classroom can be more successful.

Classroom Task Group

If a group is defined as people who relate to each other in some way, then the classroom is a group. Even though the degree of relationship may vary by classroom organisation or by class activity, there is some group interaction during the course of the class day. The classroom group is basically a task group rather than a psychoeducational or therapeutic group. The overt task of the classroom group is to master the school curriculum. The covert task is to promote personal and social growth of the students.

In many classrooms, issues of personal and social growth are seen as extraneous to the central task of the classroom, mastering the curriculum. Teachers often deal with conflicts, issues of acceptance and rejection and class cohesion only when they are forced to do so. In the inclusion classroom, these issues will surface quickly. All teachers can be more effective if they plan time and activities which will enable students to deal with issues of personal and social growth that occur in the classroom group.

Classroom Meeting

The method for group process frequently used in schools is Glasser's model of classroom meetings. Through regular and frequent meetings of the classroom group, the teacher can help the group process both task issues and personal conflict issues in non-evaluative sessions. The teacher can lead a discussion of task related issues, for instance whether or not the directions were clear or whether the resources were adequate. But the teacher can also introduce topics such as individual differences, cooperation, and decision-making which are essential to group functioning.

The class meeting is also the place to work on interpersonal conflicts that may be interfering with task completion. While the classroom meeting can provide an effective structure for group process, there will be some unique issues for the inclusion classroom.

Issues for Inclusion Classrooms

Acceptance

Before beginning the work of the classroom group, it is important for group members to feel comfortable with each other. When a student with a disability enters the classroom group, other students may focus on the "differentness" of the student and be reluctant to accept him or her into the group. The teacher can promote group cohesion by expanding the norms of acceptance to include the differences. This should be done with the entire group present, including the student with a disability. If the discussion on differences occurs without the student with a disability present, then the student with a disability is excluded from the outset.

It should be expected that acceptance will be a recurring issue for the classroom group and the student with disabilities. For instance field trips typically taken by the teacher may have to be modified to be sure the student with a disability can be included.

Commonalities of human problems

One of the benefits of all group interactions is for the individual to be aware of the commonality of human problems, thus decreasing the sense of isolation. This is particularly valuable for the student with a disability who is often isolated in the classroom group. As the classroom group recognises common problems, joys, and interests, the classroom becomes a more cohesive unit. All students feel less alone. For instance, many students can share a love of popular music or feel sad at the loss of a pet. This loss of isolation will also enhance cooperation on classroom tasks.

Task differences

When the classroom group works on a curriculum task, there is a sense of shared expectation and mastery, even though there may be individual differences in levels of achievement. The student with a severe disability, however, may need to work on a entirely different task. The teacher can help the class understand that while the task might be different for the student with a disability, he or she is still working on a learning goal which will advance the student's progress.

The class can process the ways in which all students contribute to the overall classroom group task. Or, with some tasks, the group can suggest ways that each member can best contribute to mastering the task. If the level of acceptance is high in the classroom group, then it will be easier for the class to appreciate the contribution of the student with a disability. This is another reason that issues of acceptance will need to be reprocessed throughout the life of the classroom group.

Social interaction

One of the strengths of an inclusion classroom is that it allows all students to interact socially with peers. However, often a peer friend is "assigned" to provide social interaction and some caretaking of the student with a disability. Although this may be a very positive relationship, it does not allow the student with a disability to be truly a part of the classroom group.

A more effective group work model would be to use peer helpers for a variety of students and also have different peer helpers for different tasks. Of course, it will be equally important to recognise and promote the helping skills of the student with a disability. When all students are seen as having capabilities that will help their classmates, then group cohesion is enhanced.

Immediacy

Dealing with a conflict when it occurs is an extremely valuable group process, but it may be even more important in an inclusion classroom. Because inclusion students are dealing with a new social structure, it is beneficial to discuss concerns when they arise if possible. An alternative would be to have classroom meetings at the end of each day so that issues can be discussed while still fresh. If the classroom group spends sufficient time at the beginning of the year becoming familiar with the group process and working through issues of acceptance, then students will be comfortable with immediacy.

Group Process

Many group therapy models developed from individual psychotherapy. Thus, change usually took place as a result of the therapist conducting individual therapy in the group. Hence, crucial elements for change were limited to the dynamics of the interaction between therapist and client. It is my belief, however, that for group therapy to be a unique system for change, it must escape from its earlier roots and be conceptualised as a social system. As such, it can be divided into three subsystems which will be referred to as elements: l) member, 2) leader, and 3) group. Each element is equally important in the group process.

Group therapy occurs as the result of the interactive process between the three elements. It is, therefore, important to consider all of the elements in interdependent relationship to each other. A change in one effects a change in the other. Consequently, it is incumbent upon the student of group therapy to focus upon the transactional processes occurring among and between the elements of the group.

Using linear thinking to understand the dynamic interactive process of the group will not work. Simple cause and effect relationships do not exist. This leads to the following assumption: Since therapy groups are living social systems, then regardless of where the therapist makes an intervention, its effect will be felt (have an impact upon) the rest of the system. Therefore, the therapist needs to consider how an intervention will effect not only the element being focused upon but how it will affect the other two. In essence, to touch one element is to touch all three; which in turn elicits or releases group processes.

Ways of Group Processes

Contagion

Member behaviour can elicit group processes. For instance, a member in one of our groups was talking about her sense of "emptiness." The more she talked and described her emptiness, the more involved members became by sitting forward, some crying, some touched deeply. Group behaviour would have depicted eight members "leaning" towards the talking member. The female member by talking in such a way about her "emptiness" acted as an emotional stimulant to the group eliciting the group property of emotional contagion which elicited the involvement of the group at an emotional level.

Conflict

Becoming experientially involved in a group leads automatically to conflict. It is an unavoidable consequence. Generally, conflict pervades each element at varying degrees of intensity and throughout the life stages of the group. The conflicting issues often are over such existential matters as significance, authority, autonomy, attraction, intimacy, dependence, growth, change, power, control and loss. These issues cut across and through each of the three elements. Neither the group, individual members nor the leader(s) are exempt from experiencing them. Experiencing conflict is what the leader holds in common with the members of the group. However, the difference for the leader is to have come to terms with these issues. By acknowledging or recognising their existence allows for the leader to have access to what provides for the emotional intensity that ultimately powers the therapeutic process.

Anxiety

Anxiety is a state of continual tension resulting from unsuccessful attempts to cope with internal conflicts, the roots of which lie in earlier conflicts occurring in our first group—our family of origin. When confronted by conflicts presented in a therapy group (for example a member revealing how she was abused by her father), in response, members may experience internal rumbling inside their stomachs, or a sudden sense of emptiness that will not go away. When this state of tension persists, members want to make it go away and may employ restrictive solutions such as changing the subject of group discussion, attacking the talking member, ignoring the member, detaching themselves from group or talking at an intellectual level. If successful in reducing the tension in this manner, a member interferes with another member's learning, the group's development, as well as self growth.

If on the other hand, members employ enabling solutions, such as allowing themselves to listen more openly to other members, experience the anxiety and talk about it, then anxiety can be a friend. A step in the right direction is to allow oneself to talk about feelings in response to the other members. Several assumptions can be drawn regarding the role of anxiety and its impact on group process.

First, specific issues or themes relevant to members' concerns can arouse anxiety in all the three elements. Second, either member(s), leader(s) or the group will attempt to curtail the level of anxiety by enacting restrictive solutions. Third, anxiety, in general, should be distributed among group members and not vested in one group member. Fourth, anxiety is a mobiliser of group process. The more distributed and intense the anxiety, the more evident the solutions acted out by group members. Thus, more therapeutic data and clues are available to the group therapist. A group with minimal anxiety will typically result in minimal interactions and involvement. Without tension in a group, a therapy group is rendered useless and dominated by restrictive and few enabling solutions.

Consensual validation

One of the most significant values of group therapy is that it provides an opportunity that is not available in individual psychotherapy for checking one's behaviour out with other persons and receiving feedback from the group as opposed to a single individual. The primary function of the group is to facilitate individuals to gain effective interpersonal skills for coping with their other social environments. The group provides a setting where the leader's views may be openly called to question and confronted. It is an important moment when authority figures are challenged and can simultaneously be validated as to their purpose in the group. Similarly, the group as a whole can receive validation from individual members and the leaders as to the facilitative value or lack thereof of its behaviours.

Universality

The notion that all human beings are similar is not new. Yalom has stated that once members of the group begin to interact, they soon discover that they have more in common with each other than not. This further supports why it is important for leaders to use all of the skills they can muster that will lead to getting members to interact with themselves. The more leaders are able to help members recognise the similarities of their experiences and feelings during the early stages of the group, the more they will be also facilitating group unity.

Family Re-enactment

One's family of origin and childhood conflicts never cease being an influence on current behaviour in the group. In many ways, the group resembles a family. There are the parent figures (co-leaders) who represent authority and there are the members who easily can represent siblings. It is quite common to observe and expect that members will play out old family scripts, including assuming the same that was held in the family; as well as facing unresolved issues with authority.

Recognising that this occurs and when it occurs can provide leaders with the opportunity to help the member(s) work through these old emotional impasses and unfinished family business by having the member(s) test new approaches to dealing with these issues in the group. By helping the member(s) to take a more here and now focus, the leaders can avoid engaging in the past (there and then) and have the reality of the current interaction with members (and even the leaders) receive the focus of attention.

Instillation of hope

Those who come to therapy are in all likelihood feeling hopeless. They probably have made many attempts to solve their problem(s) and all have failed. In such cases, patients seek out or find themselves in therapy and see it as a last resort. The task of the leaders is to believe in the value of their work and in the power of the group. For as members of the group manage to come to terms with their own issues, they model for others the possibilities for their own success.

2

Types of Group Counselling

Group counselling, sometimes called 'group therapy'. This means joining in a group where everyone discusses their problems together. Usually, everyone in the group is facing similar problems, but not always. The counsellor will facilitate the group and encourage people to express their feelings within it. Some people find it very helpful to learn that they are not alone with their worries.

Support Groups

Support groups are an informal resource that attempts to provide healing components to a variety of problems and challenges. An informal support outside of family, friends, or professionals often provides greater understanding, more similarity (from individuals experiencing similar life events), an opportunity for empathy and altruism, and a sense of identity for participants. Learning new ways to handle challenges, cope with changes, and maintain new behaviours are all important aspects of the support group experience.

A characteristic unique to support groups is the mutual support members are able to provide one another. This support and validation from other group members help facilitate personal growth and change in a way that individual therapy cannot. Although experts and professionals can provide support and positive direction, the mutual exchange of information between group members is a powerful experience that often induces lasting change.

Most support groups are facilitated or led by lay persons, often in conjunction with existing organisations. Support groups usually have a set meeting time (generally weekly or monthly), and an open format. Open format means that the groups are ongoing, and members have the option of attending when it is convenient for them. This is in contrast to other types of structured treatment or psycho-educational groups that may meet for a certain number of sessions, with the expectation that participants attend every meeting. The open format allows members to feel some degree of anonymity, and to participate as they are comfortable. For some people, simply attending meetings and listening to the experiences of others can be helpful.

The healing power of groups is well documented, and support groups offer many of the same therapeutic characteristics as more structured groups. These factors include: altruism (chance to help others), belongingness, universality (there are others who struggle with similar challenges), interpersonal learning, guidance, catharsis, identification, self-understanding, instillation of hope, and existential factors (such as the search for larger meaning in life). Each of these factors is directly related to the mutual support that members provide one another.

Support groups are generally less structured than psycho-educational groups or therapy groups; however, each group usually sets its own norms, rules, and schedules.

Some groups, such as AA, traditionally reserve time for individual members to discuss their own challenges and progress in front of the group. Others bring in speakers periodically to provide information about disorders or specific coping skills. However, the strength of support groups lies in its members, and their willingness to share their own experiences, challenges, and solutions in the context of the group.

In addition to these traditional, face-to-face support groups, technology has had an impact on the functioning and availability of support groups. There are many list-serves, e-mail groups, and chat groups that provide information about specific life problems, certain types of mental illness, and specific health problems. While there is always the risk of communicating with others who are not honest, many people benefit from these Internet interactions. Some individuals are actually more comfortable participating in Internet support groups due to the greater anonymity they offer.

There are a variety of problems and challenges that are addressed in support groups. Generally speaking, the severity of the symptom, as well as the phase of the illness or disorder, will determine whether participation in a support group is appropriate. For more severe types of mental illness, such as schizophrenia, or depression with psychotic episodes, a support group is probably not the optimal intervention, particularly at initial onset. After stabilisation through therapy and medication (as appropriate), a support group may offer an important addition to more formal treatment.

In these cases, the socialisation, interpersonal relationships, and social support that can be gained through the group may not be available elsewhere, and as such, it can be a very positive experience for the participant. In a group situation, a participant can learn how to express feelings in a healthy and positive way, practice assertive communication, receive feedback about appropriate and inappropriate content for conversation, receive feedback about nonverbal communication, learn new ways to ask for help from others, be able to help others, learn how to form friendships, and learn new coping skills and behaviours.

Types of Support Groups

Various types of support groups exist. Some groups provide support for very specific types of loss, illness, or life adjustment. A representative sample is listed below.

Bereavement/Grief counselling groups

Bereavement and grief counselling groups provide support to people who have experienced a loss. There are groups for people who have lost a spouse or partner, parents, children, or pets. There are specific groups for people who have lost a loved one due to homicide, suicide, SIDS, cancer, or miscarriage. These groups help individuals adjust to the death of a family member or friend, learn how to accept the loss, honour the memory of their loved one, and adjust to life after the loss.

Medical support groups

Medical support groups may be more short-term than other types of support groups, depending on the specific disorder. Some groups are formed to help patients adjust to specific treatments, such as chemotherapy or radiation, while others focus on longer-term adjustment and recovery issues, such as a breast cancer support group. These groups may have a stronger educational component to help members understand physical changes they may be experiencing as a result of their medical procedures.

Weight loss groups

Although these groups are very specific in their focus, their individual structures can vary greatly. Some weight loss support groups are actively involved in the process of losing weight, and may include monitoring of diet and exercise, while others focus on maintaining weight loss, and, therefore, may focus more on social support.

Mental health/illness support groups

These groups usually focus on specific disorders, such as bipolar or eating disorders. Members of these support groups are often at different phases in dealing with their illnesses, and, therefore, the needs and contributions of individual members may vary greatly from meeting to meeting. Most support groups are facilitated by lay persons, and usually have a set meeting time (generally weekly or monthly), and an open format. The open format allows members to feel some degree of anonymity, and to participate as they are comfortable. For some people, simply attending meetings and listening to the experiences of others can be helpful.

Family support groups

Family support groups, for families with members who struggle with any type of mental illness, provide support from other parents and children who may be feeling the same level of frustration and exasperation. Meeting others who truly understand one's experience has a very powerful effect. For many parents, participation in a support group is the first opportunity to learn that there are other parents who are experiencing the same challenges and frustrations.

Life transitions groups

Life transitions groups include divorce and aging support groups. Support groups for children of divorce also exist in many communities and schools.

Addictions support groups

Traditional addiction support groups include Alcoholics Anonymous (AA), Narcotics Anonymous (NA), and Gambler's Anonymous (GA). Many of these groups follow the traditional "12-step" programme of working through various aspects of the addiction, and, as such, are more structured than many other types of support groups.

Locations of support group

Support groups meet in many different locations within a community. Hospitals and medical centers may provide meeting locations for medical support groups. Community mental health centers, inpatient psychiatric programmes, and residential treatment centers are common locations for mental health and mental illness-related support groups. Life transition groups are often provided through schools, senior centers, and daycare centers. Bereavement groups and addiction support groups often meet in churches, community meeting rooms of local businesses, and mental health agencies.

Support groups are most successful when composed of persons close in age who are experiencing similar life challenges. Support groups are usually led by members of the group. Some support groups may be led by paraprofessionals if they are offered as part of an aftercare programme associated with a treatment facility. Support groups usually have explicit norms and expectations for member participation, such as respecting members' feelings and opinions, and coming to meetings free from drugs or alcohol. Due to the open nature of most support groups, members typically feel free to miss a session here or there, which is usually not acceptable in a treatment or therapy group.

Self-help Groups

Historically, people banded together to improve their chances for survival by pooling their social and economic resources; however, contemporary groups are more likely to organise around a theme or problem. Most self-help groups are voluntary, non-profit associations open to anyone with a similar need or interest; however, spin-off groups also exist to meet the needs of particular types of people; for example, the elderly, women, or Hispanics. Usually, groups are led by peers, have an informal structure, and are free (except for small donations to cover meeting expenses). However, professionals of various kinds lead some self-help groups.

In the past thirty years, the number of self-help organisations and groups operating in communities throughout the U.S. has dramatically risen; some organisations operate in several countries, primarily in the developed world. One of the reasons for the rapid proliferation of groups focusing on health problems may be the advent of managed health care. For individuals with insurance plans offering limited mental health coverage, self-help groups are an economical way to find emotional and social support.

Self-help Group Therapy

Because of the peer-led, informal, and democratic (as opposed to hierarchical and medical) structure, health professionals consider self-help groups for mental or emotional problems to be an adjunct to therapy. While there are therapeutic aspects associated with participation-principally, intimacy as a result of self-disclosure, personal growth in response to others' role modelling, and erosion of denial as a result of social confrontation-the primary value of contemporary groups is in the mutual aid offered by members to one another.

Though the nature of self-help groups is outside of the medical realm, doctors and therapists see participation as a way to improve the outcome related to either ongoing or future formal treatment.

Another issue arguing against considering self-help groups as a type of therapy is that the variety of groups is extensive; groups available may include advocacy groups with a focus on legal or social remedies, groups organised around housing or employment needs, and groups focusing on racial or gender issues.

Additionally, the self-help movement shares some characteristics with volunteerism and consumerism. In general, members who persevere have experience with other voluntary organisations and believe in the value of donating time and service; also, members may be thought of as consumers who participate in their own care and who have experience and knowledge of relevant goods and services.

Types of Self-help Groups

Twelve-step groups

The most popular type of self-help group is based on the Twelve Steps and Twelve Traditions of Alcoholics Anonymous (AA), founded in 1935. The Twelve Steps are a guide to recovery from alcoholism or addiction, whereas the Twelve Traditions are a code of ethics. AA and other 12-step programmes are based on the spiritual premise that turning one's life and will over to a personally meaningful "higher power," such as God or Spirit, is the key to recovery. Another essential idea is that sobriety or recovery (not cure) depends on the admission of powerlessness with respect to alcohol or the substances(s) stance(s) abused.

This idea is offensive to critics of 12-step groups, but others believe that this admission accurately reflects the contemporary view of addiction as a disease. Furthermore, people with a familial, genetic vulnerability to addiction are particularly at risk. While some studies suggest that 20% of people suffering from alcoholism will experience remission without benefit of therapy or a 12-step group, most will suffer deteriorating health and dysfunctional, if not ruined, social relationships. In other words, most alcoholics need formal therapy or an informal self-help programme to recover.

While the dropout rate for AA groups during the first three months is high, alcoholics who persevere have a good chance of attaining and maintaining sobriety or abstinence. This is especially true if the person regularly attends a home group (90 meetings in the first 90 days, slowly diminishing to two or three times per week for years thereafter) and finds an experienced and sympathetic sponsor who also is in recovery.

In addition to AA and its sister organisations, Narcotics Anonymous (NA) and Cocaine Anonymous (CA), a number of 12-step organisations exist for a variety of disorders, such as Gambler's Anonymous (GA), Schizophrenics Anonymous (SA), Emotions Anonymous (EA), and Overeaters Anonymous (OA).

Health problems and diseases groups

Self-help organisations also provide support for individuals who are ill or have health problems. For example, support exists for people coping with weight management, HIV/AIDS, multiple sclerosis, muscular dystrophy, cancer, incontinence, and for the families of individuals who suffer from these conditions. Also, support exists for people who share interests or circumstances, such as groups for women who breast-feed (LaLeche League), singles, older adults, and new parents.

Self-help groups for family members are available since illness, addiction, and distress affect the entire family. Family members may unwittingly reinforce illness or addictive behaviours, or may need help coping with the person in distress. Al-Anon, an organisation for friends and families of alcoholics, is a companion organisation to AA, as is Alateen, a programme for teenagers who have been hurt by the alcoholism of significant people in their lives. Support groups for caregivers of individuals with life-threatening or terminal illnesses, such as cancer, often meet at treatment centers and hospitals.

Online groups and clearinghouses

A growing trend in the self-help movement is the online support communities, as well as online resource centers and clearinghouses. Chat rooms, bulletin boards, and electronic mailing lists all provide convenient, around-the-clock access to peer support. Many large-scale, consumer health care web sites provide forums for discussions on numerous diseases and disorders, and major online commercial services, such as America Online (AOL), provide sites for health care and patient support. In some cases, professionals moderate online groups, although many are exclusively organised and populated by peers. There are self-help groups, such as LaLeche League, that hold some meetings online, often at their own web sites.

Features of Self-help Groups

Accessibility

Accessibility and economy are appealing features of self-help groups. Since the groups are free, organisations such as AA and NA are very cost-effective. In addition, meetings are easy to locate through local newspaper announcements, hospitals, health care centers, churches, school counsellors, and community agencies. For AA and sister organisations that encourage frequent attendance, hundreds of meetings may be held each week in large metropolitan areas. Furthermore, with the proliferation of online support communities and growth of connectivity to the Internet, self-help groups are becoming as accessible for individuals in rural areas as they are for those in large cities.

Anonymity

An important characteristic of 12-step groups is the preservation of anonymity by revealing first names only and by maintaining strict confidentiality of stories shared during meetings. Online self-help groups offer even more anonymity since the exchanges are not face to face. The virtual anonymity of online experience helps to reduce social discomfort and discrimination, or stereotyping otherwise associated with real-life perceptions of age, disabilities, race, gender, or culture.

Social support and mutual aid

Self-help groups provide an intact community and a sense of belonging. The social support and mutual aid available in a group may be critical to recovery, rehabilitation, or healthy coping. This is especially true for socially isolated people or people from dysfunctional families, who may have little or no emotional support. Participating in a social network of peers reduces social and emotional isolation and supports healthy behaviour. Group members can offer unconditional support and, collectively, are a repository of helpful experiential knowledge.

Self-esteem and self-efficacy

Self-help groups promote self-esteem or self-respect by encouraging reciprocal caring; the concept of self-efficacy, or the belief that one is capable, is promoted by reinforcing appropriate behaviour and beliefs and by sharing relevant information regarding the disease or condition. For example, there may be an exchange of information regarding how to cope with failed or disrupted relationships, about what is reasonable to expect from health care professionals, about how to manage pain or public embarrassment, about where to go and to whom for a variety of needs. In groups such as AA, self-efficacy also is promoted by sponsors who act as mentors and role models, and by encouraging rotating leadership roles.

Introspection and insight

Introspection, or contemplation, is another fundamental feature of many self-help groups, particularly for groups that follow a 12-step programme of recovery. For example, the fourth step of AA states that members make "a searching and fearless moral inventory" of themselves, and the tenth step states that members continue "to take personal inventory" and admit wrongdoing. Introspection is particularly beneficial to individuals who are not entirely aware of the moral repercussions of and motivation for their behaviour. In a sense, working through some of the 12 steps resembles the cognitive restructuring learned in cognitive-behavioural therapy (CBT), as maladaptive ideas and behaviours are transformed.

Spiritual recovery

The final step in a 12-step programme recognises that recovery entails a spiritual awakening; furthermore, recovering addicts are enjoined to spread the message to others suffering from addiction. Recovery depends on giving up both injurious self-will and denial of maladaptive behaviour, and turning to a higher power. Members are urged to seek guidance or inspiration from this higher power. For many addicts, the key to recovery is a spiritually guided movement away from self-centeredness or self-absorption, and a turning towards the "Power greater than ourselves" through prayer and meditation.

Advocacy

Some self-help groups meet to advocate or promote social and legislative remedies with respect to the issue of concern. For example, HIV/AIDS groups have lobbied for improved access to prescription drugs. Groups lobby for reforms by identifying key legislators and policy makers; they submit papers or suggestions for more equitable laws and policies to these key people. They also conduct public education programmes (including programmes meant to redress the harm of stigmatisation). There are groups that advocate for more funds for research and for improved services for people who suffer from one of many diseases or mental disorders.

The most important grass roots organisation of families and consumers of psychiatric services (former or current patients) is the US' National Alliance for the Mentally Ill (NAMI). This organisation was founded in 1979, and blends self-help with advocacy efforts for the improvement of research, services, and public awareness of major mental illnesses. Their advocacy efforts target both the federal and state levels.

Drawbacks of Self-help Groups

Advocacy vs. mutual aid

In some organisations, there is a growing overlap between self-help efforts and community development. Critics maintain that focusing on issues such as crime prevention, affordable housing, and economic development drains time and effort from social support and mutual aid. Nevertheless, some organisations continue to develop both advocacy and support.

Lack of professional involvement

The absence of professional guidance may mean that a member in need of formal psychotherapy or treatment may be discouraged from seeking professional help. On the other hand, too much professional involvement in the group may compromise the quality of mutual aid.

The "thirteenth step"

There is a well-known risk associated with attending 12-step groups termed the "thirteenth step." Women new to the groups, especially young women, are at their most vulnerable in the early stages of recovery. Male sexual predators who attend meetings take advantage of the atmosphere of intimacy and mutual trust. To cope with the possibility of sexual exploitation, young females are encouraged to attend meetings with a family member or a trusted adult, and all women are encouraged to find a same-sex sponsor.

Substituting addictions

The early months of a 12-step programme are especially difficult. Typically, an addict in early recovery either replaces an addictive substance with a new one, or intensifies his/her concurrent use of another substance.

It is not uncommon for people who are chemically dependent to also have an addictive sexual disorder. (When someone is addicted to sex, there is an intense desire to gratify sexual urges and fantasies or to behave in ways that cause clinically significant distress; sexual indulgence, often compulsive, is a major disruptive force with respect to social relationships.) In one four-year study of a treatment programme, 33% of the chemically addicted patients also were sexually compulsive. Some physicians believe that the predatory "thirteenth step" is evidence of turning from one addiction to another-in this case, addictive sexual disorder.

Members at varying stages of recovery

Another common risk is associated with the varying levels of recovery in a self-help group-that of being actively involved in the abuse of alcohol and/or drugs. Newcomers need to realise that not all members are interested in supporting their recovery, and that people in later stages of recovery may be more reliable. Furthermore, some members are required to attend by disciplinary entities, such as employers or correctional authorities.

PEER GROUPS

Peer groups are an important influence throughout one's life, but they are more critical during the developmental years of childhood and adolescence. There is often controversy about the influence of a peer group versus parental influence, particularly during adolescence. Recent studies show that parents continue to have significant influence, even during adolescence, a reassuring finding for many parents. It appears that the power of the peer group becomes more important when the family relationships are not close or supportive.

For example, if the parents work extra jobs and are largely unavailable, their children may turn to their peer group for emotional support. This also occurs when the conflict between parents and children during adolescence, or at any time during a child's development, becomes so great that the child feels pushed away and seeks closeness elsewhere. Most children and adolescents in this situation are not discriminating about the kind of group they join. They will often turn to a group simply because that group accepts them, even if the group is involved in illegal or negative activities.

Gang involvement, for example, is a common form of organised-often antisocial-peer interaction. Gangs may be based on ethnicity, sex, and/or common activity. Most youths who join gangs come from families where drug and alcohol use, financial burdens, and broken relationships are common. The need for affiliation or closeness is often greater than the need to "do the right thing" for some adolescents who feel isolated and abandoned by members of their own family. Being part of a gang provides such individuals with acceptance and security not available at home or in other peer groups.

Membership

Despite significant gains in diversity training, current studies continue to show that children are less likely to accept those who are different from themselves. The differences can be as obvious as physical impairments, or as subtle as differences in academic motivation. These rigid standards may create an atmosphere of exclusion for some children and adolescents that pushes them toward peer acceptance of any type.

Peer groups offer children and adults alike the opportunity to develop various social skills, such as leadership, sharing or teamwork, and empathy. Peer groups also offer the opportunity to experiment with new roles and interactions, similar to treatment groups, although they are less structured. It is for this reason that many children and adolescents drift from one group to another as they "find themselves," or work toward formation of their relatively permanent identity.

Aggression in Peer Groups

Although bullying and teasing have long been part of peer

group interactions, these negative behaviours have increased over the last decade, resulting in school violence in many instances. Peer groups offer children and adults alike the opportunity to develop various social skills, such as leadership, sharing or teamwork, and empathy. Peer groups also offer the opportunity to experiment with new roles and interactions, and can have positive or negative influences on an individual.

Negative peer interactions also occur more frequently following friendships or romantic relationships that have gone sour. The level of harassment that many of these children-often young women-experience is great enough for parents to become involved. In some cases, it may be necessary to move the child to another school district. A potential remediation for these negative interactions includes more active teacher involvement when negative social interactions are observed.

Peer groups can also have a positive influence-a fact many parents have known for years. Studies support parent's perceptions that the influence of friends can have a positive effect on academic motivation and performance. Conversely, experimentation with drugs, drinking, vandalism, and stealing may also be increased by interaction with the peer group.

Since schools are often the site of negative peer interactions, school personnel have a unique opportunity for effective intervention. Many schools have peer-mediation programmes, in which students are encouraged to resolve conflicts on their own without the use of violence or aggression. School counsellors also organise groups within the school to handle various problems, including providing social skills training and empathy training.

Peer groups often provide an example for negative and harmful behaviours. Cluster suicide is one such example. When a teen realises that someone he or she knew has attempted or has committed suicide, the teen may see suicide as a viable option for him- or herself as well. For this reason, schools and local media should exercise caution when reporting such tragedies. Care must be taken not to portray the suicide glamorously or mythically.

When parents try to protect their children by telling them to stay away from certain friends, they should realise that sometimes this only encourages them to seek out negative role models. Parents should be supportive of their child and redirect their child's activities to more positive and prosocial peers and events. A trusted adult friend, such as a scout leader or a respected coach, may be an important part of the redirection effort.

Children and adolescents without strong family connections, or at least a positive connection with other adults in their life, face a higher risk of negative influence from peer groups. If the child or adolescent has not been able to form bonds with positive peer groups, it is more likely they will be perceived as distant and different from their peers, making them feel more like outsiders. Lower standards of acceptance often exist in less positive peer groups, making it easier for people to join. Unfortunately, many such groups often engage in self-destructive and anti-social activities.

3 Group Therapy

Group therapy is a form of psychotherapy in which a small, carefully selected group of individuals meets regularly with a therapist. The purpose of group therapy is to assist each individual in emotional growth and personal problem solving.

Group therapy encompasses many different kinds of groups with varying theoretical orientations that exist for varying purposes. All therapy groups exist to help individuals grow emotionally and solve personal problems. All utilise the power of the group, as well as the therapist who leads it, in this process.

Unlike the simple two-person relationship between patient and therapist in individual therapy, group therapy offers multiple relationships to assist the individual in growth and problem solving. The noted psychiatrist Dr. Irvin D. Yalom in his book *The Theory and Practice of Group Therapyidentified* 11 "curative factors" that are the "primary agents of change" in group therapy.

All patients come into therapy hoping to decrease their suffering and improve their lives. Because each member in a therapy group is inevitably at a different point on the coping continuum and grows at a different rate, watching others cope with and overcome similar problems successfully instills hope and inspiration. New members or those in despair may be particularly encouraged by others' positive outcomes.

A common feeling among group therapy members, especially when a group is just starting, is that of being isolated, unique, and apart from others. Many who enter group therapy have great difficulty sustaining interpersonal relationships, and feel unlikable and unlovable. Group therapy provides a powerful antidote to these feelings. For many, it may be the first time they feel understood and similar to others. Enormous relief often accompanies the recognition that they are not alone; this is a special benefit of group therapy.

Components of Group Therapy

An essential component of many therapy groups is increasing members' knowledge and understanding of a common problem. Explicit instruction about the nature of their shared illness, such as bipolar disorders, depression, panic disorders, or bulimia, is often a key part of the therapy. Most patients leave the group far more knowledgeable about their specific condition than when they entered. This makes them increasingly able to help others with the same or similar problems.

Altruism

Group therapy offers its members a unique opportunity: the chance to help others. Often patients with psychiatric problems believe they have very little to offer others because they have needed so much help themselves; this can make them feel inadequate. The process of helping others is a powerful therapeutic tool that greatly enhances members' self-esteem and feeling of self-worth.

Corrective Recapitulation

Many people who enter group therapy had troubled family lives during their formative years. The group becomes a substitute family that resembles-and improves upon-the family of origin in significant ways. Like a family, a therapy group consists of a leader (or coleaders), an authority figure that evokes feelings similar to those felt toward parents. Other group members substitute for siblings, vying for attention and affection from the leader/parent, and forming subgroups and coalitions with other members. This recasting of the family of origin gives members a chance to correct dysfunctional interpersonal relationships in a way that can have a powerful therapeutic impact.

Basic Social Skills

According to Yalom, social learning, or the development of basic social skills, is a therapeutic factor that occurs in all therapy groups. Some groups place considerable emphasis on improving social skills, for example, with adolescents preparing to leave a psychiatric hospital, or among bereaved or divorced members seeking to date again. Group members offer feedback to one another about the appropriateness of the others' behaviour. While this may be painful, the directness and honesty with which it is offered can provide much-needed behavioural correction and thus improve relationships both within and outside the group.

Imitative Behaviour

Research shows that therapists exert a powerful influence on the communication patterns of group members by modelling certain behaviours. For example, therapists model active listening, giving nonjudgmental feedback, and offering support. Over time, members pick up these behaviours and incorporate them. This earns them increasingly positive feedback from others, enhancing their self-esteem and emotional growth.

Interpersonal Learning

Human beings are social animals, born ready to connect. Our lives are characterised by intense and persistent relationships, and much of our self-esteem is developed via feedback and reflection from important others. Yet we all develop distortions in the way we see others, and these distortions can damage even our most important relationships. Therapy groups provide an opportunity for members to improve their ability to relate to others and live far more satisfying lives because of it.

Group Cohesiveness

Belonging, acceptance, and approval are among the most important and universal of human needs. Fitting in with our peers as children and adolescents, pledging a sorority or fraternity as young adults, and joining a church or other social group as adults all fulfill these basic human needs. Many people with emotional problems, however, have not experienced success as group members. For them, group therapy may make them feel truly accepted and valued for the first time. This can be a powerful healing factor as individuals replace their feelings of isolation and separateness with a sense of belonging.

Catharsis

Catharsis is a powerful emotional experience-the release of

conscious or unconscious feelings-followed by a feeling of great relief. Catharsis is a factor in most therapies, including group therapy. It is a type of emotional learning, as opposed to intellectual understanding, that can lead to immediate and long-lasting change. While catharsis cannot be forced, a group environment provides ample opportunity for members to have these powerful experiences.

Existential Factors

Existential factors are certain realities of life including death, isolation, freedom, and meaninglessness. Becoming aware of these realities can lead to anxiety. The trust and openness that develops among members of a therapy group, however, permits exploration of these fundamental issues, and can help members develop an acceptance of difficult realities.

Historical Overview of Group Therapy

Group therapy in the United States can be traced back to the late nineteenth and early twentieth centuries, when millions of immigrants moved to American shores. Most of these immigrants settled in large cities, and organisations such as Hull House in Chicago were founded to assist them adjust to life in the United States. Known as settlement houses, these agencies helped immigrant groups lobby for better housing, working conditions, and recreational facilities. These early social work groups valued group participation, the democratic process, and personal growth.

In 1905, a Boston physician named Joseph Pratt formed groups of impoverished patients suffering from a common illness-tuberculosis. Pratt believed that these patients could provide mutual support and assistance. Like settlement houses, his early groups were another forerunner of group therapy. Some early psychoanalysts, especially Alfred Adler, a student of Sigmund Freud, believed that many individual problems were social in origin. In the 1930s Adler encouraged his patients to meet in groups to provide mutual support.

At around the same time, social work groups began forming in mental hospitals, child guidance clinics, prisons, and public assistance agencies. A contemporary descendant of these groups is today's support group, in which people with a common problem come together, without a leader or therapist, to help each other solve a common problem. Group therapy offers multiple relationships to assist an individual in growth and problem solving. In group therapy sessions, members are encouraged to discuss the issues that brought them into therapy openly and honestly. The therapist works to create an atmosphere of trust and acceptance that encourages members to support one another.

Types of Therapy Groups

Psychodynamic Therapies

Psychodynamic theory was conceived by Sigmund Freud, the father of psychoanalysis. Freud believed that unconscious psychological forces determine thoughts, feelings, and behaviours. By analysing the interactions among group members, psychodynamic therapies focus on helping individuals become aware of their unconscious needs and motivations as well as the concerns common to all group members. Issues of authority (the relationship to the therapist) and affection (the relationships among group members) provide rich sources of material that the therapist can use to help group members understand their relationships and themselves.

Phenomenological Therapies

Until the 1940s virtually all psychotherapy was based on psychoanalytic principles. Several group therapy approaches were developed by psychoanalytically trained therapists looking to expand their focus beyond the unconscious to the interpretations individuals place on their experiences. Underlying this focus is the belief that human beings are capable of consciously controlling their behaviour and taking responsibility for their decisions. Some phenomenological therapies include:

— *Psychodrama*-developed by Jacob Moreno, an Austrian psychiatrist, this technique encourages members to play the parts of significant individuals in their lives to help them solve interpersonal conflicts. Psychodrama brings the conflict into the present, emphasising dramatic action as a way of helping group members solve their problems. Catharsis, the therapeutic release of emotions followed by relief, plays a prominent role. This approach is particularly useful for people who find it difficult to express their feelings in words.

— *Person-centered therapy*-a therapeutic approach developed by the psychologist Carl Rogers. Rather than viewing the therapist as expert, Rogers believed that the client's own drive toward growth and development is the most important healing factor. The therapist empathises with the client's feelings and perceptions, helping him or her gain insight and plan constructive action. Rogers's person-centered therapy became the basis for the intensive group experience known as the encounter group, in which the leader helps members discuss their feelings about one another and, through the group process, grow as individuals. Rogers emphasised honest feedback and the awareness, expression, and acceptance of feelings. He believed that a trusting and cohesive atmosphere is fundamental to the therapeutic effect of the group.

— *Gestalt therapy*-In the 1940s Frits Perls challenged psychoanalytic theory and practice with this approach. Members take turns being in the "hot seat," an empty chair used to represent people with whom the person is experiencing conflicts. The therapist encourages the client to become aware of feelings and impulses previously denied.

Behaviour Therapies

Behaviour therapies comprise a number of techniques based upon a common theoretical belief: maladaptive behaviours develop according to the same principles that govern all learning. As a result, they can be unlearned, and new, more adaptive behaviours learned in their place. The emergence of behaviour therapies in the 1950s represented a radical departure from psychoanalysis. Behaviour therapies focus on how a problem behaviour originated, and on the environmental factors that maintain it. Individuals are encouraged to become self-analytical, looking at events occurring before, during, and after the problem behaviour takes place. Strategies are then developed and employed to replace the problem behaviour with new, more adaptive behaviours.

An important offshoot of behaviour therapy is cognitive-behavioural therapy, developed in the 1960s and 1970s, which is the predominant behavioural approach used today.

It emphasises the examination of thoughts with the goal of changing them to more rational and less inflammatory ones. Albert Ellis, a psychologist who believed that we cause our own unhappiness by our interpretations of events, rather than by the events themselves, is a major figure in cognitive-behaviour therapy. By changing what we tell ourselves, Ellis believes we can reduce the strength of our emotional reactions, as well.

Individuals that share a common problem or concern are often placed in therapy groups where they can share their mutual struggles and feelings. Groups for bulimic individuals, victims of sexual abuse, adult children of alcoholics, and recovering drug addicts are some types of common therapy groups.

Individuals that are suicidal, homicidal, psychotic, or in the midst of a major life crisis are not typically placed in group therapy until their behaviour and emotional states have stabilised. People with organic brain injury and other cognitive impairments may also be poor candidates for group therapy, as are patients with sociopathic traits, who show little ability to empathise with others.

Building Therapy Groups

Therapy groups may be homogeneous or heterogeneous. Homogeneous groups, described above, have members with similar diagnostic backgrounds (for example, they may all suffer from depression). Heterogeneous groups contain a mix of individuals with different emotional problems. The number of group members typically ranges from five to 12.

The number of sessions in group therapy depends upon the group's makeup, goals, and setting. Some are time limited, with a predetermined number of sessions known to all members at the beginning. Others are indeterminate, and the group and/or therapist determines when the group is ready to disband. Membership may be closed or open to new members. The therapeutic approach used depends on both the focus of the group and the therapist's orientation.

In group therapy sessions, members are encouraged to discuss the issues that brought them into therapy openly and honestly. The therapist works to create an atmosphere of trust and acceptance that encourages members to support one another. Ground rules may be set at the beginning, such as maintaining confidentiality of group discussions, and restricting social contact among members outside the group.

The therapist facilitates the group process, that is, the effective functioning of the group, and guides individuals in self-discovery. Depending upon the group's goals and the therapist's orientation, sessions may be either highly structured or fluid and relatively undirected. Typically, the leader steers a middle course, providing direction when the group gets off track, yet letting members set their own agenda. The therapist may guide the group by reinforcing the positive behaviours they engage in. For example, if one member shows empathy and supportive listening to another, the therapist might compliment that member and explain the value of that behaviour to the group. In almost all group therapy situations, the therapist will emphasise the commonalities among members to instill a sense of group identity.

Self-help or support groups like Alcoholics Anonymous and Weight Watchers fall outside of the psychotherapy realm. These groups offer many of the same benefits, including social support, the opportunity to identify with others, and the sense of belonging that makes group therapy effective for many. Self-help groups also meet to share their common concern and help one another cope. These groups, however, are typically leaderless or run by a member who takes on the leader role for one or more meetings. Sometimes self-help groups can be an adjunct to psychotherapy groups.

Individuals are typically referred for group therapy by a psychologist or psychiatrist. Some may participate in both individual and group therapy. Before a person begins in a therapy group, the leader interviews the individual to ensure a good fit between their needs and the group's. The individual may be given some preliminary information before sessions begin, such as guidelines and ground rules, and information about the problem on which the group is focused.

Therapy groups end in a variety of ways. Some, such as those in drug rehabilitation programmes and psychiatric hospitals, may be ongoing, with patients coming and going as they leave the facility. Others may have an end date set from the outset. Still others may continue until the group and/or the therapist believe the group goals have been met.

The termination of a long-term therapy group may cause feelings of grief, loss, abandonment, anger, or rejection in some members. The therapist attempts to deal with these feelings and foster a sense of closure by encouraging exploration of feelings and use of newly acquired coping techniques for handling them. Working through this termination phase is an important part of the treatment process.

Individuals who are emotionally fragile or unable to tolerate aggressive or hostile comments from other members are at risk of dropping out, as are those who have trouble communicating in a group setting. If the therapist does not support them and help reduce their sense of isolation and aloneness, they may drop out and feel like failures. The group can be injured by the premature departure of any of its members, and it is up to the therapist to minimise the likelihood of this occurrence by careful selection and management of the group process.

4 Counselling Approach

Living In Balance (LIB) Counselling Approach

The Living In Balance (LIB) counselling approach is specifically oriented for the group setting and utilises techniques that draw from cognitive, behavioural, and experiential treatment approaches, with an emphasis on relapse prevention (RP). The LIB manual uses didactic education and instruction, group process interaction through role plays and discussion, daily relaxation and visualisation exercises, informational handouts, videotapes, and group-oriented recreational therapy exercises. Both counsellors and clients may find the detailed organisation and educational orientation of the LIB manual to be unfamiliar or uncomfortable at first, but over time both counsellors and clients are likely to find that the manual provides a solid foundation for treatment that can be used in a flexible clinical context.

There are 36 LIB sessions, each covering one specific topic. The major addiction-related topics include RP, drug education, and self-help education. Physical health issues addressed include nutrition, sexually transmitted diseases (STDs), HIV/AIDS, dental hygiene, and insomnia.

Psychosocial topics include attitudes and beliefs, negative emotions, anger and communication, sexuality, spirituality, and the benefits of relationships. In addition, there are sessions on money management, education and vocational development, and loss and grieving. Each session contains a combination of PE, experiential, and group process and RP components.

Throughout the LIB programme, clients learn to monitor their own feelings and behavior and use relaxation and visualisation techniques in the self-assessment and goal-setting processes. Throughout the programme clients learn to become actively involved in treatment-learning how to conduct self-assessments and actively implement coping and RP skills. One of the strongest emphases in the LIB programme is to teach clients how to become their own relapse preventionists. This includes teaching them about the psychological and physiological components of addiction and recovery, and the various types of interventions and "life skills areas," in which ongoing intervention is necessary.

Addiction Professionals

The LIB approach is designed to provide addiction professionals with a practical guide to conducting a series of 36 group treatment sessions for people who have drug use problems. The intent of the LIB programme is to save addiction professionals time and expense by providing pre-prepared sessions, similar to a teacher's lesson plans. In many treatment programmes, the scope and quality of information and education provided to clients depend on the skills of the counsellors working in the programme at any given time. Thus, the scope of expertise may be limited, and the accuracy of the information may vary from counsellor to counsellor.

In contrast, the developers of the LIB manual identified the primary issues that should be addressed in treatment and then created therapeutic sessions to address those issues. Thus, the LIB manual provides information about an extensive array of issues of importance to treatment and recovery. Also, the individual sessions of the LIB manual are based on current research in addictive behaviours and RP.

Clients

Clients in treatment place significant emphasis on the following needs:

1. Information about treatment and recovery.
2. Skills to handle feelings and emotions.
3. Information about preventing relapse.
4. Practical living skills.
5. Open confrontation when engaged in denial or other types of distorted thinking or behaviours.

Thus, the goal of the PE approach of the LIB manual is to provide education, information, and experiences that will show people how to lead healthy and productive lives without using alcohol, cocaine, or other drugs. To achieve this goal, the LIB manual presents accurate information about drugs of abuse, RP, self-help programmes, medical and physical health, emotional and social wellness, sexual and spiritual health, daily living skills, and vocational and educational development. The information is not presented as a long, boring lecture. Rather, each session is divided into manageable segments.

Each of the 36 treatment sessions detailed in the manual allows for approximately 90 minutes of counsellor interventions, presentations, or client training and includes sufficient time for questions. After each segment is a question-and-answer session that lets clients intensively interact with the counsellor. During most sessions, there are written assignments that engage clients in an interactive exercise with the information. When appropriate, there are role-play exercises that encourage intense interaction and discussion among clients. Each session has one overriding goal with several specific client objectives.

Clients are guided through a series of exercises that allow them to develop their own personal goals and objectives for each of the major life areas covered in the various treatment sessions. Using a combination of cognitive, relaxation, and visualisation skills, clients are asked to identify, visualise, and take active steps toward their personal goals and objectives.

Rationale Mechanism of Action

The basic rationale of the LIB model is that persons addicted to drugs develop a sense of imbalance in major areas of life functioning. Continuous drug use generally impairs a person's physical health, emotional well-being, social relationships, work performance, and other major areas of functioning. Recovery involves regaining a reasonable balance in these critical areas. Balance in the major areas of life allows clients to free themselves from their addiction to drugs and provides protection against relapse to drug use. The concept of "living in balance" is essentially a broad, holistic approach to RP.

RP is the single most important component of the LIB programme. The first section of the programme is devoted primarily to developing RP skills; RP sessions are scheduled strategically throughout the programme. The understanding and skills that clients develop in these segments are meant to be used throughout the LIB programme on a daily basis. The LIB programme approach to RP is based in large part on a cognitive-behavioural model of RP developed by Marlatt and Gordon.

In this model, the former drug user confronts a high-risk situation for which he or she has no effective coping response. According to the model, high-risk situations can occur for many reasons, including social pressure to use drugs, negative emotions, and, less frequently, withdrawal symptoms and positive emotions. The lack of a coping response combined with positive expectancies for the initial effects of the drug in the situation greatly heighten the risk of a slip. Regarding relapse, the model suggests that "a person headed toward a slip makes numerous small decisions at the time which, although seemingly small and irrelevant at the time they are made, actually bring the individual closer to the brink of the slip. A chain of small decisions can lead, over time, to relapse".

The biopsychosocial LIB approach to this patterning and slip chain is to rework it-to offer clients information about high-risk physical, social, and psychological situations and the potential impact of "small decisions"; to offer clients training in coping responses and stress reduction strategies; and to guide clients down alternative paths to pleasure and other life satisfactions. LIB RP helps clients:

— Identify situations that trigger cravings.

— Understand the chain of events, including "small decisions," that lead from trigger to drug use.

— Disrupt the chain at an early point.

— Cope with triggers by using thought-stopping, visualisation, and relaxation techniques.

— Develop immediate alternatives to drug use.

— Develop a long-term plan for full recovery.

RP is viewed as a fundamental component of treatment and is consequently emphasised in the LIB manual by the use of repeated RP sessions. These sessions are intended to reinforce critical RP concepts and allow clients the opportunity to discuss and process difficult situations that they face in their daily lives that could easily lead to slips or full-blown relapse. Intensive use of visualisation exercises is intended to strengthen RP skills and aid in forming and reinforcing personal goals.

Agent of Change

The agent of change in the LIB model is multidimensional, involving interaction among the group counsellor, the client, and the other group members. Although a highly structured format is provided for conducting the group sessions, the counsellor is encouraged to utilise his or her personal skills and experience to engage and involve the clients in treatment. In addition, group interaction is highly encouraged, and many of the activities such as role plays, discussions, and games are designed to facilitate group interaction and elicit emotional responses and social bonding. Intrapersonal techniques such as visualisation, meditation, and even homework exercises are also extensively used, as they require personal responsibility and discipline on the part of the client for maximum benefit.

Causative Factors of Drug Addiction

In the LIB approach, addiction is viewed as a

biopsychosocial process that not only handicaps an individual's functioning but also may destroy the cohesiveness of family and community relationships. Biopsychosocial processes refer to the inherited biological vulnerabilities, psychological predispositions, and pervasive social influences that converge to both form and perpetuate addictive behaviours.

Biological factors

Although related evidence is equivocal regarding biological contributions to addictive behaviours, it has been a common belief that some people are born with a genetic predisposition for developing an addiction when exposed to psychoactive drugs. Following chronic drug use, all people experience a severe biological (neurochemical) imbalance. Drug hunger, intoxication, and withdrawal are all manifestations of drug-induced imbalances of biologic homeostasis.

Psychological factors

Some people begin their drug use to diminish potent emotional and psychiatric symptoms. In turn, addiction causes a variety of psychological problems; drug use and withdrawal can cause numerous psychiatric symptoms Even recovery can cause severe emotional turmoil Importantly, addiction causes distortions in thinking suc as denial, minimisation, and projection.

Social factors

Various environmental factors increase the likelihood exposure to specific drugs. For instance, certain drugs more frequently used within certain cultures, and cer

drugs are more easily found in certain geographic areas. For many people, drug use occurs in the context of a social network. In addition, addiction frequently causes severe disruptions in people's social lives. Various social and environmental factors can also contribute to the triggering of drug hunger and relapse. Addiction is further viewed as a chronic, disabling condition in which relapses are common.

Each client's unique history and evolution of addiction must be evaluated at each of these levels, so that an effective treatment plan can be tailored to the client's needs, strengths, and weaknesses. The more comprehensive the intervention, the more successful the outcome is likely to be. Because addiction affects multiple areas of clients' lives, treatment efforts should address all major areas of living. The LIB programme takes a nonjudgmental approach to addiction and lifestyle issues. In general, clients are viewed as people with a compulsive disorder that often overwhelms good intentions and willpower. Clients can be taught RP techniques to avoid a re-emergence of the symptoms of addiction: compulsion, loss of control, continued use despite adverse consequences, and relapse.

Developments of LIB Models

The initial development of the LIB model drew some of its basic concepts from the Neurobehavioral Treatment Model, particularly regarding the RP strategies. Some of the materials and handouts on RP were adapted from information in the Matrix Center's manual. The primary difference between the Matrix neurobehavioral model and the LIB model is LIB's emphasis on structured group counselling. The neurobehavioral model is a more flexible

approach utilising a combination of individual, family, and group therapies, with much less emphasis on group processing and experiences.

The LIB model and the neurobehavioral model are also similar to other cognitive-behavioural approaches such as those developed for alcohol treatment as described in Treating Alcohol Dependence: A Coping Skills Training Guide. This approach also emphasises client mastery of skills that will help them maintain abstinence from alcohol and other drugs. Clients are instructed to identify high-risk situations that may lead to relapse and analyse the external events, the internal cognitions, and the emotions that may precipitate relapse.

Clients then develop plans and practice skills to cope with these situations, thoughts, and feelings, using various problemsolving, role-play, and homework exercises. Many of these basic RP concepts and techniques were based on the original work of Marlatt and Gordon and Gorski and Miller. LIB uses these concepts in a simple and direct manner and expands on this approach to incorporate a comprehensive holistic view toward lifestyle change.

Dissimilar Counselling Approaches

The 12-step addiction treatment model is most commonly used in addiction treatment programmes. Its approach is grounded in the concept of addiction as a spiritual and medical disease, and its content is consistent with the 12 steps of AA. In addition to abstinence, a major goal of this treatment approach is to foster each client's commitment to participation in AA and Narcotics Anonymous (NA) self-help groups. Therapy sessions generally follow a similar format that includes symptoms inquiry, review and reinforcement for AA/NA participation, and introduction and explication of each session's theme within the AA/NA philosophy (acceptance and surrender to the higher power, moral inventories, and sober living.) Material introduced during treatment sessions is often complemented by reading assignments from AA and NA literature.

The LIB approach is not completely dissimilar to the 12-step approach and in fact incorporates many of its concepts and encourages participation in its self-help programmes. LIB, however, places a much greater emphasis on learning and practicing critical RP skills and on strengthening major areas of a client's life to reinforce protection against relapse. Like 12-step programmes, LIB encourages spiritual exploration (finding a source of involvement greater than the self). But the primary focus remains on making informed decisions in everyday life that help the client regain balance and prevent relapse to drug use.

Format

The LIB counselling approach is designed for group counselling in any type of drug treatment setting. It can be used as a primary modality over a period of 4 to 6 months, in combination with other treatment approaches (e.g., medical and psychosocial modalities), and for varying lengths of time. LIB incorporates a self-help approach and encourages participation in self-help programmes that the client determines most suitable to his or her needs and personal philosophy.

Modalities of Treatment

The LIB programme is designed for use in a group counselling format. Groups may range in size from 5 to 20, but a group numbering between 12 and 15 has been found to provide a good balance between individual attention and group processing. LIB can be combined with other modalities such as individual and family psychotherapy and can be modified in accordance with the needs of specific treatment programmes.

Ideal Treatment Setting

The LIB programme can be used in drug abuse treatment settings as the core treatment or as an adjunct treatment strategy, depending on the clinical setting, level of care, and type of programme. The LIB programme can be used in all levels of care:

— Inpatient or outpatient.

— Intensive outpatient.

— Partial hospitalisation.

— Continuing care and aftercare.

— Evening or weekend programmes.

The LIB programme can be used in a variety of programme types:

— Freestanding.

— Hospital based.

— Community based.

— Corrections based.

— Counselling centers.

— Methadone treatment.

— Therapeutic communities.

— Halfway houses.

— Therapists in private practice.

The LIB programme has been designed by a multidisciplinary team of healthcare professionals for use by trained addiction professionals. In many treatment programmes, the LIB manual will be used primarily by addiction counsellors and therapists. Some treatment programmes may choose to have various healthcare professionals lead some of the group treatment sessions in their areas of expertise. Physicians may lead the sessions on STDs, nurses may lead the sessions on physical well-being, and nutritionists may lead the session on nutrition.

Duration of Treatment

The LIB manual is divided into 36 sessions. Each session lasts about 2 hours and is held 3 days a week over a 12-week period (allowing for holidays and special events), or less frequently over a longer period of time. Specific sessions have been identified for different treatment settings, populations, and levels of care. The LIB programme is designed so that clients can enter into the programme at any session and continue the programme until all of the intended sessions are completed.

Modality of Treatments

The LIB programme can be used as the primary modality of treatment in an intensive outpatient programme or in combination with other common modalities. Hoffman and colleagues found that when LIB groups were conducted 5 days a week, adding individual and family psychotherapy contributed little to increasing either the number of days or the number of sessions attended in outpatient treatment for cocaine abuse. However, when LIB groups were offered only twice a week, adding individual and family psychotherapy significantly increased the number of sessions attended.

LIB has also been used effectively in methadone treatment programmes, particularly during the early phases. When used properly within the confines of a comprehensive treatment programme, medication (including methadone) is viewed by the authors of the LIB concept as a useful adjunct in helping clients regain and maintain a life of balance and sobriety. LIB is also currently being used in residential treatment programmes and specialised programmes for drug-abusing women.

Self-Help Programmes

The LIB programme views the 12-step programmes of AA, NA, and Cocaine Anonymous (CA) as important components in the treatment and recovery process for cocaine addiction. The LIB manual introduces clients to this and other self-help programmes and encourages clients to attend self-help meetings during and following the formal treatment programme. In addition, the manual embraces alternative recovery self-help groups and promotes spiritual awareness. The LIB manual also incorporates 12-step programme references and examples throughout the text. Each client must find his or her own sources of support and fulfillment that extend beyond the limits of a treatment programme and professional counselling.

Characteristics and Training of Counsellors

The effectiveness of any treatment model or counselling approach is determined by the personnel who use the model or deliver the programme. The background, training, education, and experience of LIB counsellors are critical to the effective use of this approach. Counsellors who have more clinical training and related experience will be more capable of using various components of the model to effectively address the myriad issues that arise during a treatment session.

Educational Requirements

The LIB model is designed to be used by anyone who has experience as a drug abuse counsellor or who has other professional addictions training. Certification as an addictions counsellor is also recommended but not required. Although an individual who has a high-school diploma would have adequate reading comprehension skills to use this model, it is recommended that the individual have an associate's, bachelor's, or master's degree. This additional education and training would enhance an individual's ability to fully understand the materials being presented and draw on his or her own experiences in developing certain concepts and ideas that are presented in the various sessions. Although the LIB manual is written in simple, easy-to-understand language, some of the concepts and exercises actually have very complex underpinnings.

Training, Credentials, and Experience

Ideally, the individual using the LIB approach should have extensive training in the area of addictions. This level of training is encouraged because it provides a conceptual foundation and the skills requisite for any treatment modality. National certification as an addictions counsellor is recommended; however, being a certified addictions counsellor is not a requisite for using this counselling model. The effectiveness of the model is contingent on the counsellor's knowledge of the addictions field, his or her knowledge of various treatment techniques, and his or her experience in using those skills and techniques that are critical for working through the denial and resistance that are characteristic of a drug-using population.

Recovery Status

The LIB counselling approach can be used by counsellors who have had a recovery experience or who have never used drugs. A counsellor's recovery status is a complex issue that needs to be addressed in counsellor training and supervision. It has been found that counsellors who are recovering addicts can sometimes use their personal experiences to help illustrate certain points and that they have a greater sensitivity to some clients' responses and concerns. However, it is also important that the recovering counsellor have mastery of RP skills and practice them in his or her own life, because a counsellor should serve as an example of a person who is leading a relatively balanced life.

Counsellors in recovery should use their own judgment, preferably in consultation with a supervisor, about when, how, and whether to reveal their own personal recovery experiences. This self-disclosure should be made only with a clear understanding of the potential benefits to the client. At no time should a counsellor use the group sessions to discuss or resolve his or her own personal problems.

Personal Characteristics of Counsellor

While ideal counsellor characteristics have not been clearly identified, some basic qualities that are useful in any counsellor are sensitivity, a nonjudgmental attitude, and a genuine desire to help people struggle through some of the problems that led to their use of alcohol or other drugs. A counsellor using the LIB model should be able to lead group discussions and provide basic instruction for those topics that require didactic presentation. Other personal characteristics that are helpful are openness, honesty, an ability to set appropriate limits, and a capacity for demonstrating caring while confronting behaviours that are inimical to the goals and objectives of the model.

The counsellor should be skilled at confronting the client in denial. One of the major impediments to successful treatment is a client's denial of his or her addiction. This denial expresses itself in many ways and many forms, from outright denial of having a drug problem to expressions of disinterest in the various topics and an unwillingness to discuss certain subjects. The counsellor needs to be able to describe the behavior (e.g., avoiding certain topics, expressing denial), demonstrate the pattern of behavior as it appears, and relate the behavior to the defence mechanism of denial as it expresses itself in the course of treatment. In addition, the counsellor must be adept at pointing out both strengths and weaknesses in a client.

Periodically during group sessions, a clear effort should be made to identify strengths that the client has demonstrated over the course of treatment and point out areas where continued growth is necessary. The major emphasis, however, should be on noting strengths. It is very important that a counsellor using the LIB model be prepared. Lack of preparation will lead to an inaccurate or stifled presentation of information. The information is not intended to be read verbatim; it should be presented in a personalised and meaningful way. The counsellor must understand and be familiar enough with the material to allow him or her to concentrate on group processing and individual needs and concerns.

The LIB approach to group work uses virtually all of the skills and intervention strategies that would normally be used in a group setting. Standard group counselling techniques and interventions are generally appropriate within the LIB model, although the approach relies more heavily on PE rather than psychotherapeutic strategies. The LIB model is designed to identify problems and develop skills and strategies for addressing them. For this reason, the counsellor might refrain from using techniques designed to encourage the client to relive traumatic and unresolved childhood and adult experiences or attempt to treat comorbid psychiatric disorders directly in the group setting.

Nevertheless, materials, films, and role-play exercises are likely to elicit strong emotional reactions, and it is appropriate to acknowledge and discuss these feelings. Should intense, unresolved emotional issues arise in a group session, the counsellor might suggest that the client address these issues in an individual session. The counsellor should use his or her judgment in determining whether to seek the assistance of a trained psychologist or psychotherapist. The counsellor should also discourage detailed discussions of drug use that may glorify use or stimulate or trigger a conditioned craving for drugs.

However, the counsellor should be careful to reframe the discussion in terms of understanding the precipitants and associations to drug use and should curtail detailed discussions or storytelling not directly pertinent to learning RP skills. If the counsellor comes to believe that the discussion may have triggered a craving in a client, the matter should be addressed immediately, and concrete solutions should be identified for disrupting the pattern of behaviour that would likely lead to drug use.

Proposed Supervision

The primary goal of supervision is to help the counsellor

use his or her clinical skills to present the information contained in the LIB manual in a manner that engages the group and facilitates individual recovery. To achieve this goal, the supervisor should:

— Help the counsellor develop his or her basic counselling skills, such as reflective listening and reframing.

— Develop the counsellor's skill in the use of the model, particularly in the area of RP training.

— Assist in evaluating the emotional state of the group and in helping determine when to use various sessions to meet the treatment needs of the group.

— Assist in dealing with difficult issues in group process, such as clients who dominate the discussion or focus excessively on drug use or drug-related behavior.

The supervisor must know the level of clinical expertise of each counsellor under supervision. The supervisor needs to know the extent to which the counsellor is comfortable using confrontation, demonstrating empathy, and encouraging supportive group interactions. Also recommended is use of the case conference approach, where LIB counselling staff can develop alternative strategies for problem resolution as each case is reviewed in depth. Finally, the supervisor must observe group sessions to be able to provide behavioural and skills-based feedback to counsellors. These observations are critical in helping counsellors develop and enhance their clinical skills.

Relationship of Client and Counsellor

The relationship between client and counsellor permits the client to use the counsellor as a sounding board and to appreciate and value the insights and observations the counsellor makes with regard to the client's progress. Therefore, developing a strong relationship, one of caring and concern, is imperative to the counsellor's ability to intervene effectively in the life of the client in a manner that is helpful to recovery.

In some cases, the counsellor is clearly an educator by virtue of the PE approach of the model. The counsellor educates the client about matters related to drug abuse, both in terms of the pharmacological or biological impact on the body and the impact that drugs have on other areas of life. In this educator/teacher role, the counsellor begins to provide the client with knowledge about the impact of alcohol and other drug use, which will enable the client to make informed decisions regarding his or her use of these drugs.

The counsellor also plays the role of therapist in providing clients with a valuable resource for understanding and changing their behaviours in a healthy, productive way. The counsellor helps clients understand their feelings about particular areas of their lives and helps them work through their struggles. This model discourages the counsellor from being an adviser to the client. The model itself is one that is geared toward empowering the client to take charge and independently make decisions regarding his or her life.

The LIB model requires the counsellor to do most of the talking. In most sessions, the counsellor initially uses a didactic approach, imparting information regarding a particular subject area. The counsellor must then facilitate group discussion and interaction. In a 90-minute session, the counsellor will spend about 30 minutes either offering some instruction verbally or engaging the client in some kind of experiential process, where instruction and guidance are offered. The remaining hour of the session is generally devoted to the interactive component of the programme, where the client is encouraged to express feelings, reactions, or thoughts regarding a particular topic area.

Because LIB requires the counsellor to take the lead and guide clients through a structured set of group experiences, the counsellor is highly directive. The primary objective of these group experiences is to empower clients to make informed decisions regarding their use of alcohol and other drugs and to begin to lead a more balanced and healthy lifestyle.

Therapeutic Alliance

The quality of the client-counsellor relationship can significantly enhance the impact of any technique used in working with an individual or group. Thus, the most effective counsellor develops an alliance with the client that is characterised by honest and clear communication, explicit empathy, respect for the individual, and a clear treatment objective. The treatment contract is one way of developing such an alliance. The contract should establish explicit goals for the individual and the group, clearly state what the counsellor will do to help the group or individual achieve those goals, and articulate behavioural expectations or group rules (e.g., not interrupting, being on time, not leaving the group session unless absolutely necessary).

In situations where the alliance is poor, the counsellor needs to explore, with the supervisor, interventions that might strengthen that relationship. For example, if gender is an impediment to establishing a working therapeutic relationship, the counsellor needs to determine the efficacy of discussing the issue with the client in an individual session. If the counsellor decides to discuss the issue with the client, the counsellor should gently state that the client appears to have some discomfort or negative feelings toward the counsellor that might be interfering with the client's participation in the group process. The counsellor should not be threatening, accusatory, or defensive, but should be accepting of the client's feelings and should try to clarify any wrong perceptions. The counsellor should be aware that the client may be reacting to previous negative experiences with treatment. In any case, the counsellor should convey concern for the client and work toward improving the alliance.

The LIB programme was originally designed for an inner-city, predominantly minority, cocaine-abusing population in an intensive outpatient treatment programme. Nevertheless, it is applicable for a wide range of drugs of abuse, including heroin and alcohol, and for clients from a wide range of cultural and economic backgrounds. The LIB manual was designed to be universally applicable across various cultural and ethnic backgrounds. Its biopsychosocial and holistic approach to treatment assumes that living a balanced life is a fundamental objective of all people, regardless of race, culture, or ethnic background. Establishing physical, emotional, social, and spiritual well-being is considered to be a central objective in the process of recovery from drug addiction for all individuals.

The role of culture and ethnicity is also a critical element of the recovery process. An addiction counsellor's cultural sensitivity is a prerequisite to providing effective treatment. Unless the counsellor is aware of and sensitive to the cultural and ethnic issues and concerns of clients in treatment and understands socioeconomic and racial factors, his or her effectiveness will be severely restricted and potentially counterproductive. The counsellor must have knowledge of and empathy for the ethnic and cultural experiences, perceptions, and values of his or her clientele.

Clients best suited for the LIB programme are those who are comfortable participating in a group. LIB generally does not involve intense group confrontation or indepth psychodynamic processing; however, the sensitive nature of some of the issues covered requires a minimum level of comfort with group interaction. If a client is not comfortable in this situation, it may be possible for him or her to participate in individual counselling until a later phase of treatment when he or she is more ready to join an LIB group.

The LIB programme is generally suitable for clients of all ages (late teens to elderly persons), although it would be ideal to limit participation in each group to specific age ranges so that peers of similar age can address concerns relevant to their experience. LIB can be used with mixed-gender groups and with men-only and women-only groups. (Same-sex groups are preferred and generally recommended when dealing with issues of sexual and emotional abuse .) LIB can be tailored to any ethnic or cultural subgroup and be implemented with users of different types of drugs, and it can include sessions on alcohol and nicotine addiction. LIB has been used with a variety of different groups (e.g., Latino alcoholics, African-American pregnant and postpartum crack-using women, Caucasian methamphetamine users, and mixed ethnic/cultural heroin users).

The LIB programme can be used in any type of drug treatment or social service setting and is ideal for use with special populations (e.g., welfare to work, criminal justice, public housing, mental health) where drug abuse problems exist. There are specific sessions that the LIB manual suggests using when dealing with some of the key counselling issues for these populations. LIB complements the 12-step approach, provides information about various self-help-oriented programmes, and encourages participation in those programmes.

The LIB group counselling approach may not be suitable for clients who are uncomfortable in a group setting. Initial discomfort is common and natural given the implicit pressure to reveal and expose personal feelings to a group of strangers. However, this discomfort quickly diminishes for most clients. Some clients who have high social anxiety, who are extremely introverted, or who have difficulties with logical thought processes may not respond well to this group counselling format. In addition, some of the more educational components of the programme may be difficult for clients who have very low reading or cognitive abilities. Although most of the materials are discussed aloud and assistance is available for those who need help with written assignments, clients must have the ability to understand the concepts presented in order to benefit from the programme.

The LIB programme has been successfully implemented with a diverse group of cocaine-abusers, which included court-referred and dually diagnosed clients. The only notable limitation, as mentioned earlier, is that clients must be able to attend meetings and comprehend the concepts conveyed. Clients with psychotic disorders, for example, may not be suitable candidates for participating in the LIB programme if they have difficulty functioning in a group setting or in comprehending the information in an objective manner. However, these clients may be suitable if their severe psychiatric symptomatology is adequately controlled through adjunctive treatments and they can function comfortably in a group setting.

Assessment Protocol

An assessment protocol that measures the specific domains covered in the LIB programme has not yet been developed. The intensive treatment approach has so far been deemed superior in encouraging higher levels of client participation in treatment, and both approaches appear superior to many prior reports of comparative treatment findings with crack smokers. Measures such as the Addiction Severity Index (ASI), a commonly used measure in addiction research, can be used in assessing the following parameters: client demographics, treatment history, lifestyle and living arrangements, alcohol and other drug use, HIV and AIDS risk behavior, illegal activities and criminal histories, employment status, and mental and physical health status.

Format and Content

The LIB manual provides a detailed description for 36 treatment sessions in the form of instructional text similar to a teacher's lesson plan. The information is prepared so that counsellors can gain a thorough understanding of the topic and present it in manageable segments. In addition to the written instructional text, each session includes:

— *Handouts for clients.* Questionnaires, assignments, exercises, and lists of additional resources for appropriate topics for clients.

— *Presentation transparencies.* "Visuals," which are key words and important phrases and concepts presented in each session.

— *Videotapes.* Nine videotapes that focus on many of the session topics.

— *Daily progressive relaxation and visualisation exercises.* Progressive relaxation exercises that teach clients stress reduction skills.

— *Relaxation and visualisation audiotape.* Substituted for counsellor-led relaxation exercises.

The LIB manual, with emphasis on PE, was designed to educate clients on how to conduct self-assessments. The manual focuses on specific "life areas," in which prolonged drug use has had a negative impact. The various topics covered in the LIB programme are summarised below.

— *Visualisation, self-assessment, goal setting, planning, and self-monitoring.* Clients are offered training in relaxation techniques, goal setting, planning, and self-monitoring. They are instructed in and practice using relaxation exercises as an RP tool to help them intervene in stressful situations and when they experience cravings for alcohol, cocaine, or other drugs. They learn how to set personal goals for recovery, how to conduct self-assessments in key life areas, how to deal with life improvements, and how to practice life skills. Training is repeated throughout the sessions.

— *Drug education.* Clients learn about the psychological and physiological components of addiction and recovery and about the neurophysiology involved in addiction and recovery. They also learn in great detail about the psychological processes involved in craving and relapse. Clients participate in discussions about the classical conditioning that occurs surrounding internal and external "triggers" or conditioned cues that may elicit craving experiences and in role-play-related interventions and learn techniques to diminish the power of conditioned cues.

— *Relapse prevention*. Clients take part in intensive RP sessions, where they practice RP skills in "process sessions." This is where clients talk about their current risk factors and intervention efforts to prevent relapse and where they can role-play responses to high-risk situations. Clients learn about the operant and classical conditioning that occurs and how specific cues (e.g., people, places, and things; certain times of day; special smells and sounds) that they associate with prior drug use can lead to craving their drug of choice and relapse unless they actively plan and intervene. They also learn how to eliminate or extinguish such learned associations and practice specific skills in coping with high-risk situations. Planning for coping with high-risk situations, generating social support for abstinence, and learning how to cope with unanticipated stress or temptations are all central to these sessions.

— *Self-help education*. Clients are encouraged to use specific intervention skills such as implementing stress management techniques and eliciting social support (recovery groups such as AA, NA, or one of the more recently established secular groups such as Rational Recovery. The primary goal is to ensure that, as an adjunct to treatment, clients have abstinent role models to help them cope during high-risk times and provide them with a form of ongoing support after they have completed the formal treatment provided by the LIB programme.

— *Sexually transmitted diseases*. As part of the session on STDs, clients are given information on various diseases and risk factors for each. An additional session, devoted to HIV and AIDS, emphasises the risk of contracting HIV within an addict population and explains risk reduction strategies. The various high-risk behaviours that cocaine, alcohol, heroin, and other drug addicts engage in (risky and unsafe sex practices and needle sharing) are discussed, and the importance of reducing all risk behavior for HIV infection is explained. HIV and AIDS testing and treatment are also reviewed.

— *Physical well-being*. The negative impact of illicit drugs and alcohol, cigarettes, and prescription drugs is discussed; diet, exercise, and overall health maintenance (i.e., medical and dental care and personal hygiene and appearance) are emphasised. Group discussions on these topics as they relate to drug addiction and to a more positive lifestyle are integrated into several sessions.

— *Emotional well-being*. Specific areas that are emphasised in this area include depression, anxiety, fear, anger and hostility, and guilt and shame. There are also group discussions of these topics as they relate to emotional problems and drug abuse and to the manner in which emotional strengths and problems can influence other life areas.

— *Social well-being*. Specific topics covered include interactions with friends and relationships with lovers/spouses, parents and parent figures, siblings, offspring, and other significant others (SOs). Discussions in these sessions can show how relationships can be linked to drug abuse and how behaviours associated with drug abuse can be changed. The role that SOs may play in enabling drug use and the peer pressure that can generate drug-abusing behavior and relapse are discussed. Modelling, behavior rehearsal, and role playing are significant components for teaching clients.

— *Sexuality*. The topic of sex and drugs is included in several sessions. Sexual dysfunction, sexual abuse, sexual addiction, sexual behavior as a risk behavior for relapse, and healthy sexuality are discussed, along with the effects of drugs in inhibiting sexual behavior.

— *Education and vocational development opportunities*. Specific topic areas include reading and language skills, math and technical skills, possible alternatives for further education, relating education to employment goals, and learning for pleasure. This is an opportunity for the client to review his or her vocational history, interests and aptitudes, and skills training and preparation to gain, maintain, and enhance employment.

— *Daily living skills*. Specific topics include transportation, housing, legal assistance, financial assistance, and budgeting.

— *Spirituality and recovery*. The concept of spirituality, defined globally in the religious sense and also in terms of simply having some sense of purpose, direction, or meaning in life, and its potential utility for recovering addicts is discussed. Other topics include the role of spirituality in providing a positive meaning for life; ritual and symbolism; peace of mind; and beyond the self.

— *Grief, loss, and recovery*. Each is addressed to educate clients about the relationships between addiction and loss. Responses to loss are addressed, and the process of grief and factors that can affect grief is reviewed. The stages of grief are characterised, and strategies to deal with important losses, including the use of support services, are covered.

— *Parents and parenting*. Sessions are designed to assist clients in understanding the basic needs of children that they or other caregivers must address, as well as the needs that parents and other caregivers have when parenting children. Developmental stages of children are reviewed, and clients are taught how they can help children in meeting their developmental tasks. The issues that children face at different developmental levels are also addressed. Clients are shown specific parenting skills such as communication skills, problemsolving, and positive reinforcement.

Common Clinical Problems

The LIB approach is not immune to the usual assortment of clinical problems. During the admission process, clients should be informed of programme policies and the consequences of violating those rules. Invariably, clients will miss sessions, arrive late, or come to treatment under the influence. As with any other programme, there should be established policies and procedures governing these matters. When problems are addressed in the context of the LIB programme, they provide valuable opportunities for behavioural interventions within the group and with the client. Following are some examples of how these problems might addressed.

Lateness

The programme policy should establish lateness as an issue that is discussed in the context of the group. A pattern of lateness affords an opportunity for the counsellor to help the group examine how the same faulty planning process that leads to lateness can contribute to relapse. Also, the group can explore the impact of an individual's lateness on his or her social relationships. The group can actually develop a plan to resolve the lateness problem, which can allow clients to develop skills that can be applied to other life situations.

Missed Sessions

Missed sessions are to be expected; therefore, each programme should develop a policy that is consistent with its treatment philosophy. In the context of the LIB approach, however, the focus of the intervention should be on the frequency of, and reasons for, missed sessions. Because a client's absence has an impact on the dynamics of the group, the counsellor should use the issue to help group members identify their emotional response to the repeated absences of a member. Also, it is probable that some absences will be a response to feelings that surfaced in the previous session. This presents a perfect opportunity for the counsellor to educate the group about the relationship between feelings and behavior.

Attending Sessions Under the Influence

A client who comes to a session under the influence of alcohol or other drugs should not be allowed to participate. If a client's condition is such that there is concern about allowing the individual out into the community, the client should be held in a separate room until he or she is capable of leaving the programme safely. As soon after the incident as possible, an individual session should be held to review what took place and help the client develop a more effective plan for abstinence. If the incident took place in the presence of the group, it should be the focus of an RP session. Otherwise, the counsellor should use his or her clinical judgment regarding the appropriateness of discussing the incident in the group session. These issues should be addressed in a manner consistent with the philosophy and orientation of the treatment programme.

Although policies and procedures are necessary and should be applied with consistency, their application should be tempered by the clinical needs of clients. It is the authors' opinion that a blanket sanction for all clients, with no consideration for individual differences and individual growth patterns, is problematic and does not allow for maximising the individualisation of the treatment programme. An effort should be made, therefore, to impose sanctions in a manner appropriate to the level of development of the particular client.

Denial, Resistance, or Poor Motivation

It is unrealistic to expect every client to enter treatment acknowledging the severity of his or her addiction and be highly motivated for change. In fact, the very essence of treatment is confronting and overcoming the client's denial, resistance, and lack of motivation. Therefore, an effective model of treatment must incorporate a variety of strategies to address these fundamental barriers to long-term recovery. Following are strategies employed in the LIB model to address these clinical issues.

Because LIB uses a PE approach to treatment, all of the sessions provide a means for confronting a client's denial. For example, the RP sessions help clients identify thoughts, feelings, and situations that trigger their use of alcohol and other drugs. This process helps teach clients how triggers relate to relapse. Another aspect of denial can be the tendency of clients to blame their drug abuse on others. In the sessions addressing social well-being, clients are guided through an examination of the key relationships in their lives. This examination helps clients understand how their responses to problems in their relationships are reflective of the decisions they make and that their problems cannot be used as rationalisations for their drug abuse. This approach works in many areas of a client's life, such as social relationships, emotional well-being, and other areas where denial may be a factor that prevents the client from moving forward in treatment.

Resistance is another area frequently seen in the treatment sessions that merits considerable time and attention. Clients express their resistance in numerous ways: through arriving late to individual or group sessions, distracting behavior during group sessions, challenging and argumentative behaviours, and so on. The LIB programme has built in some mechanisms for dealing with resistance: the use of relaxation and visualisation exercises and the communication and presentation of information by way of videotapes, handouts, and role plays.

In some cases, the counsellor should use the topic of a particular session to help clients begin to examine how their behavior may reflect resistance to treatment. In light of factors such as denial and resistance, it is imperative that counsellors use the group to assist in their interventions. Interventions made by the counsellor carry significant weight, but when the group can help a member recognise denial or resistance by observing the member's behavior and sharing their own experiences with denial or resistance, such continued intervention can have a tremendous impact on the client's overcoming resistance to treatment.

Poor motivation is another area that will inevitably need to be addressed during the course of treatment. It is usually best for the counsellor to discuss an apparent lack of motivation with the client outside of the group sessions. It may be determined that there are other clinical issues that are upsetting the client or interfering with his or her ability to concentrate or participate in the group sessions. Once the lack of motivation is openly acknowledged, the client will be faced with the choice of engaging in treatment or discontinuing participation.

5

Integrated Approach to Group Counselling

Social and Labour Market Integration Approach

Social and labour market integration represents a considerable challenge for youth in general and an even greater challenge for at-risk youth. Indeed, youth who have experienced numerous difficulties in personal and social development encounter significant obstacles integrating themselves into society and into the labour market. Ouellette and Doucet observed that the personal, social, educational, and vocational characteristics of at-risk youth resembled traits in individuals exhibiting weak personal and vocational identities which could contribute to integration difficulties of at-risk youth. This led to the development of a model of the factors contributing to social and labour market integration and a programme to develop personal and vocational identity.

Model of Social and Labour Market Integration

The model of social and labour market integration consists of three main dimensions:

1. *Psychovocational dimension*: This is the heart of the model and consists primarily of: personal identity - Erikson's first six stages (trust, autonomy, initiative, industry, identity, and intimacy); vocational identity - Havighurst's first four stages (identification with a worker, development of basic work habits, development of an identity as a worker, and becoming a productive person).
2. *Sociopsychological dimension*: It subsumes the psychovocational dimension and consists of family, peers, school, work, and media networks.
3. *Sociological dimension*: It subsumes the sociopsychological dimension and consists of economic, political, cultural, geographic, and demographic factors.

The model was verified, via focus-group interviews, by professionals working with at-risk youth, by employers who employ these youth, and by individual interviews with a sample of at-risk youth.

Counselling Young Offenders for Rehabilitation and Employment

Counsellors and educators of young offenders and other at-risk youth need to be aware of how various orientations carry different, and sometimes opposing, beliefs and assumptions which create confusion over prevention and intervention practices in community and school. Four primary models are evident:

1. *Societal change model*. Youth crime is a product of society and its institutions (family, community, school) and is beyond the control of the individual.

Intervention in this model addresses issues of poverty and inequity in the community rather than "correcting" the individual.

2. *Welfare model.* The young offender is assumed to be have psycho/social deficiencies that cause offending behaviour. Intervention provides appropriate therapy to rehabilitate the individual.

3. *Justice model.* Society must be protected from offenders. Individuals commit crime of their own free will, must be held responsible, and might pay the penalty set by society under due process.

4. *Crime-control model.* Societal order is maintained through laws that punish wrong doing, achieve retribution through punishment, and deter criminality by threat of punishment. Youth are no exception.

Perspectives of Alternative Development

Research over the past decade offers renewed promise for counselling interventions that prepare young offenders to be productive members of society. Programmes typically stress the prevention of behaviours that lead to re-offending. Most behaviours and attitudes don't directly lead to successful employment, however, they can be thought of as preparatory. Research is demonstrating what works and also what leads to failure:

— "Quick fix" programmes do not work. Programmes must be offered over months, not weeks, and of sufficient intensity to change entrenched behaviours and attitudes. Follow-up "booster" sessions contribute to programme effectiveness.

— Programmes that employ single aims or strategies do not work. Youth offending has no single cause and the young offender population is far from homogeneous.

— Successful programmes are multi-faceted. They use multiple strategies (e.g., skills, problem-solving, self-monitoring, aggression control), have multiple targets (e.g., individual, peers and home), and have multiple specific goals that typically generalise over time and across settings.

— Programme effects can be missed; programmes may be labelled as "failures" if evaluation is faulty. Simplistic evaluation designs and unreliable criteria (e.g., recidivism) cannot address the complexity of short-term and long-range outcomes.

— Programmes do not work when those who offer them do not believe in their efficacy. Successful programmes can fail because of cynicism among those who implement and administer them.

— Lack of programme fidelity is a common cause of failure. Successful programmes are often complex, a reflection of the complex causes of youth offending. If they are not delivered as designed and those implementing them are not well trained, successful programmes can fail.

Effective Programmes

Effective programmes for young offenders and other at-risk youth typically take place in the community (e.g., schools, open-custody residences, group homes, social agencies). The following examples represent the types of promising programmes being applied in Canada. All are multi-faceted, intensive, relatively long-term, and systematically evaluated. They do not have a specific career focus, but go beyond simply finding jobs for at-risk or offending youth. These programmes address skill training both in preparation for work and in job maintenance.

The BreakAway Company is a highly structured, 12-week programme for residential or school use, based on cognitive-behavioural instruction principles. It simulates a work place in which students are treated as "employees" and group identity is fostered. The teacher/counselor is their "supervisor." they receive a token salary and bonuses, negotiate contracts, work cooperatively, receive information through Company memos, attend staff meetings, and do job shadowing and short-term placements.

The Company "products" are reflected in its objectives: discovering one's own abilities and job-related skills, and learning cognitive-behavioural strategies that address problem-solving, interpersonal relations, and aggression control. Evaluation of the programme over 2 years indicates that most students learn the strategies and apply them in various settings. In 6 to 8 month follow-up interviews, participants reported such observations as: "You just stop and think before you do everything now. It's just natural now..."; "Now I think out problems in slow motion."; "I learned how to control my anger... think about it, sit down, and say, 'Look what you're doing wrong'."

Multisystemic treatment is a 2-4 month community-based programme that addresses the causes of delinquency. The focus is on the family system as the center of a network that includes siblings, peers, and school. Emphasis is on preserving the family and developing effective social-cognitive skills.

Online Support Groups

Computer technology is now altering the traditional ways people handle stress. More people participate in online support groups on such thematic topics as alcoholism, eating disorders and depression which provide privacy from the comfort of home. Online support groups can range from serving as one therapeutic component of a comprehensive mental health treatment plan to serving as the sole support system. They attract a broad variety of members who may previously have avoided peers and their traditional support system. Satisfied members report feeling validation and support while dissatisfied members express frustration caused by technology problems and by the absence of visual, auditory and interpersonal cues.

Components of Online Support Groups

— *Access*. Online support groups can be accessed through use of a computer and modem in conjunction with an Internet service provider (ISP) such as America Online (AOL). Once connected through an ISP, online support groups may also be reached through Internet portals (e.g., Yahoo) or through specialised websites.

— *Format*. Online support groups can function in real time (i.e., synchronous group) and through newsgroups (i.e., asynchronous groups):

— *Synchronous Groups*. Groups are interactive. Members correspond anonymously using text-based communication in real time. These groups use contrived screen names (i.e., pseudonyms), meet at a scheduled time to encourage consistent participation and convene for one hour on average.

— *Asynchronous Groups*. Members post messages and questions twenty-four hours in newsgroups to a specific member or to the general membership. This format allows members to send and retrieve messages at their convenience and regardless of their time zone.

— *Group Leader*. Groups are led by hosts who may be a mixture of mental health professionals and non-professionals, depending on the site. Hosts function as resource persons rather than online counsellors. They use human relations skills to assist members in expressing feelings, disseminate information and make referrals to helplines, self-help resources, traditional support/self-help groups, local counselling centers, crisis centers, and hospice centers. They also recommend links to other online support groups, mental health web sites and fee-based cyber mental health services.

Strengthening Online Support Groups

— *Increased Access to Support*. Online support groups reduce the sense of isolation for those who reside in underserved or remote locations, are housebound, need additional support between traditional support groups or counselling sessions, or seek anonymity. Internet access at a library, after-school programme or community center enables a person with limited financial resources to participate as an equal member without financial resources becoming a barrier.

— *Adjunct to Counselling*. Online support groups can function as an effective therapeutic adjunct to counselling services for members who require more support than counselling offers and/or more frequent support than counselling provides. A member can join several free online support groups between counselling sessions and seek support without experiencing additional expenses.

— *Therapeutic Factors*. Members of online support groups benefit from Yalom's seven therapeutic factors.

Through a combination of therapeutic factors, the potential for growth, change and social experimentation contribute to the group's cohesion and perceived helpfulness. For example, the factor of "universality" unites people as they share similar thoughts, feelings, fears and/or reactions with their cyber community. Others struggle too, and this is not always evident to people in distress.

— *Specialised Online Support Groups.* Specialised groups can connect people who need someone with whom they can communicate honestly and openly without regard to geographic boundaries. Groups dedicated to specific topics, age groups or gender groups can be formed.

— *Privacy.* Groups give members the privacy to seek support and information about behaviour that might be perceived as a stigma and thereby become a barrier to seeking counselling and/or information. However, to ensure privacy, a member should minimise participation in an online support group at an employer's computer, during the lunch hour for example, because the employer may be legally entitled to monitor transmissions and computer activity.

Drawback of Online Support Groups

— *Differing Stages of Group Development.* Groups are open continuously to new membership. In addition to new members joining an established group, other online members may log on or log off at any time during a session. Such fluctuations in membership make it difficult for online groups to engage in the typical group phases of warm-up, action and closure or to maintain the working stage of group development for extended periods. This limitation reduces the efficacy of online support groups as a sole support source for some members.

— *Limited Feedback*. The lack of face-to-face contact obscures vocal intonations and verbal and non-verbal cues, including body language and expressions of emotion. Limited feedback may require changes in a member's habitual patterns of interaction and thinking in order to overcome this limitation. Dissatisfied members typically cite limited feedback as a disincentive to participate.

— *Crisis Management*. The successful resolution of an emotional crisis in cyberspace is challenging. Limited feedback and the lack of identifying information complicate the assessment and referral process.

— *Anonymity Breaches*. Steps are taken to maintain the anonymity of each member and the confidentiality of group dialogue. For example, the host discourages the exchange of identifying information and personal communication between members. However, anonymity can be breached. Members must consider the risk of a breach in anonymity before joining.

— *Host Competency*. Requirements for hosts vary among websites, portals and ISPs. Hosts should state their professional qualifications (or indicate none) at the beginning of each session, or during orientation, while not divulging their true identity.

— *Quality Control*. The quality of online support groups is inconsistent. Each sets its own standards and procedures. The new user should try several groups in search of the best fit.

— *Members with Limited Language Skills.* Members with an expressive or receptive learning disability or with language limitations (such as English as a second language) may be frustrated by the rapid pace and multiple dialogues, and consequently, may be frustrated by text-based communication. Furthermore, members may be challenged in communicating feelings and thoughts clearly to others. In a text-only format with limited interpersonal feedback, communicative misunderstandings are common for all members and this could be exacerbated for the member with limited language skills. We recommend software programmes that convert spoken words to text and vice versa.

— *Ethical and Legal Concerns.* The hosting of and participation in online support groups raises some ethical and legal questions that currently remain unanswered. Currently, it is unclear if the online support group is considered a cyberspace mental health service. However, several mental health professional organisations and licensing boards have begun to grapple with cyberspace ethical and legal issues.

— *Hoax Perpetuations.* People with unscrupulous motives can deceive an online support group. Hoaxes tend to occur because members are anonymous or lack an emotional commitment to the cybercommunity.

Technological advances can make online support groups somewhat comparable to face-to-face support groups while avoiding the inconveniences associated with gathering at a specific location. However, some of the benefits of privacy and anonymity that members currently enjoy and find unique about online support would be compromised to various degrees.

Drug Abuse Prevention

During the past decade much has been learned about school-based drug prevention programming. We now know that effective programmes are comprehensive, begin intervention efforts early, project a clear no-use message, contain different strategies for different populations, and coordinate their programme with a broader community-wide prevention effort. More light has also been shed on the strengths and weaknesses of specific programme components, including curricula. Though drug prevention curricula assessment has been difficult, evidence is mounting that curricula based on the Social Influence Model (SIM) is especially effective in changing student drug-use attitudes and behaviour.

Research has also shown that allowing students to take an active role in prevention programme delivery strengthens the programme as well as boosting the self-esteem and academic performance of the students who assist. Because of these advantages, more and more schools are enlisting the skills and enthusiasm of trained "peer leaders" to lead other students through SIM-based drug prevention curriculums.

Peer leaders have been used by student services professionals since the mid-1960s. Peer leaders have assisted school counsellors and administrators in providing support for fellow students with special needs such as academic (tutoring), social (orienting new students), physical (aiding handicapped students), or emotional (leading support groups). Both the growing strength of the self-help movement, and the diminishing resources available to schools for assisting students, have made peer leader programmes appealing.

Selection of peer leaders has been done in a number of ways, although most programmes do not restrict participation to high achievers or student leaders. In fact, serving as a peer leader has been shown to have a transforming effect on the school performance of underachieving and alienated youth. Once selected, peer leaders go through a special training programme to develop strong communication and decision-making skills.

Specific benefits of a peer leader programme include: (1) freeing up time for teachers and counsellors to perform other tasks, (2) providing strong role models for other students (peers are more effective as role models than adults), (3) creating a less threatening counselling environment where students can share attitudes and experiences that they might not wish to discuss with an adult, and (4) strengthening the self-esteem of peer leaders by providing them with leadership experience and an opportunity to play a meaningful role in the lives of others.

Social Influence Model (SIM)

Based on the knowledge that social pressures play a major role in shaping behaviour, especially the behaviour of youth, the Social Influence Model (SIM), or Peer Influence Model as it is sometimes called, seeks to strengthen students' awareness of and resistance to the external pressures exerted by friends, family, and the media, and to internal pressures such as low self-esteem that can lead youth to drug use. Prevention curriculum based on SIM dispenses objective information about drug use (within the context of a clear no-use philosophy), examines drug use attitudes and behaviours, and gives social resistance skill training.

Using Peer Leaders in SIM

A variety of SIM curriculum delivery modes exist including printed materials, presentations, media announcements, posters, games, surveys, movies, and computer programmes. One SIM approach especially conducive to the use of peer leaders is discussion and resistance skill training groups where students can sort out together assumption from fact and learn and practice assertiveness skills that will help them successfully negotiate their way through the various social situations in which their behavioural choices are challenged.

Discussion/resistance skills training has become popular because it capitalises on adolescent needs for competence, autonomy, recognition, and fun, and addresses social isolation that can lead to feelings of alienation and delinquent behaviour. Skills targeted for improvement are:

1. cognitive awareness
2. goal setting
3. problem identification and management
4. decision making
5. communication, including assertion and refusal skills.

Peer leaders lead fellow students through a specific drug prevention curriculum that includes group discussion, question/answer and writing exercises, and individual and group role playing. During these exercises students challenge each others' beliefs, try out new social skills, and provide important emotional support to one another that can extend beyond the group session.

Using peer leaders to deliver SIM-based drug prevention curricula has many benefits. By giving youths an opportunity to help and learn from each other, student-led SIM curricula address the internal needs of youth for personal efficacy and self-worth, while building valuable skills in identifying and effectively resisting social pressures to use drugs. To be effective, peer-led SIM programming efforts should:

1. be supervised by well-trained adults capable of modelling the desired skills;
2. be based on demonstrated needs;
3. represent the social composition of the school and community;
4. be interactive and experiential; and,
5. provide peer leaders with extensive training and opportunities for skill renewal.

Prevention Programme Administrators

In addition to their use in directing group discussion/ resistance skill training groups, peer leaders also serve as prevention programme administrators: assessing school needs, selecting appropriate programmes, and coordinating programme implementation and assessment. They also have taken the leadership in developing alternative drug-free school and community activities. Peer leaders in some school districts have served as instructors for younger students, teaching them about the hazards of drug use while indirectly serving as powerful role models. Others have encouraged peer leaders to establish and coordinate student-run businesses to give youth more skills and greater experience with assuming adult responsibilities.

6

Creative Techniques in Group Counselling

Before dealing with specific creative group counselling techniques, let us examine the advantages and possible disadvantages of using groups.

Groups Are Good/Not So Good

Good

— High productivity
— More effective decisions
— Socialization of positive values
— Emotional life is enhanced
— Better conflict resolution
— Social competencies enriched
— Cooperation is needed

Not So Good

— Groups take more extreme positions

— Diffusion of responsibility

— Anonymity can result in negative behaviour

— More impersonal

— Collective panic

— Victims of distorted views of leaders

— Forced conformity

Groups can bog down during the early stages (initial/ transition) and even in the midst of the working stage. Following are a few reasons why some groups don't work very well, some conditions that will result in group member change and some helpful forces in group work.

Why Some Groups Don't Work Very Well

— Not using creative techniques to get and hold the attention of the group members

— Not supporting techniques with theory

— Not focusing the group sessions sufficiently

— Reflecting too many feelings and listening to far too many long stories

— Lack of leader courage and creativity

— Insufficient group member movement and involvement

— Dawdling rather than focusing sessions

— Insufficient attention to different learning styles (visual, auditory, experiential, etc.)

Conditions for Changing Groups

— Instilling Hope

— Universality

— Imparting Information

— Altruism

— Socializing

— Modeling

— Cohesiveness

— Catharsis

Helpful Forces in Group Work

— Commitment

— Responsibility

— Attractiveness

— Security

— Tension

— Power

— Expectations

— Acceptance

— Belonging

— Group Norms

— Hope

— Feedback

Techniques for the Initial Stage

— physical setting

— getting acquainted

— trust-building

— focusing

Techniques for the Transition Stage

— roleplay

— role reversal

— dealing with difficult members

— conflict resolution

Techniques for the Working Stage

— intense emotions

— moving to the real world

— rounds

— processing

— contracting

Techniques for the Termination Stage

— rehearsing

— projecting the future

— handling goodbyes

— reunion fantasy

— closing party

Types of Creative Techniques

Everyday articles

— Hammer

— Cards

— Tapes

- Chairs
- Rubber bands
- Rearview mirror
- Paper cups
- Paper money

Drawing and writing

- journals
- genograms
- favorite animal drawing
- favorite item in the room
- "What would that do for me?"
- pot bound drawing
- epitaph

Stories and metaphors

- egograms
- exception finding
- strokes
- stories you loved at an early age
- favorite movie
- ratings
- ABC disputing
- Moses in the wilderness

Group member movement

— walking in circles

— standing in a corner

— moving with (or not) others

— feeling pulled

— empty chair movement

Group facilitators are not just part of a group to listen, but are there to help group members fulfill their goals. The Impact Therapy model of Ed Jacobs suggests that to be more effective leaders need to use:

— multisensory appraoches,

— motivational devices,

— marketing, and

— maps.

Group leaders can not just talk and listen but need to use visual, kinesthetic, and auditory approaches to engage group members. There is a much better chance of motivating clients to make changes when they are engaged through a wide variety of creative techniques. Leaders need to market themselves and convince group members that they can be helpful to group members. And, finally, group leaders should use maps (a flipchart or whiteboard) so that group members can write things down. It stays with them longer.

7

Counselling for Teenagers and Parents

In most instances, teenage pregnancy has been viewed solely as a woman's issue, with the adolescent father regarded as a shadowy, unknown figure—more a culprit than a potential contributor to either the mother or his offspring. School and agency counsellors must continue to offer programmes to support young mothers and their children, but this forgotten half of the teenage pregnancy problem cannot continue to be overlooked. Recently, the plight of the unwed, teenage father has begun to gain attention.

Young men in American society generally are expected to have it all together or to pretend that they do. Too often, unwed teenage fathers have been stereotyped as callous, "macho studs" who are interested only in their own pleasure. Because of these stereotypes, counsellors, educators, and others did not believe that the young men recognised their need for help or that they would participate in programmes designed to assist them. Studies now show that most teenage fathers do not have it all together and are just as confused, afraid, and anxious as the young women they impregnate.

Maximising a Life Experience Group

Most teenage fathers care about what happens to their children and need to be given the opportunity to explore their concerns and feelings; however, they do not usually ask for help on their own. The Maximising a Life Experience (MALE) programme was developed to focus on a different set of the three Rs: Rights, Responsibilities, and Resources. The general goals were to help the young men understand their emotional rights (to express feelings and concerns and receive emotional support) and responsibilities, as well as their legal rights and responsibilities, and to learn about available resources. The specific objectives for the programme were to help the teenage fathers:

1. Learn more about themselves and better understand their feelings about their present situation.
2. Understand their legal and emotional rights and responsibilities.
3. Recognise that pregnancy cannot be dismissed as an accident.
4. Obtain factual information about reproductive biology, contraception, and sexually transmitted diseases.
5. Identify and explore their present and future options.
6. Learn how to solve problems and make sound decisions.
7. Realise what resources are available and how to use them.

Male Group

The eight group participants were enrolled in a suburban high school with a student population that was primarily

Black and from lower socioeconomic levels. The young men, two of whom were expectant fathers, were between 15 and 18 years old and had academic averages that ranged from a B to a D. About half of them hoped to continue their education after high school graduation. The average age of first sexual activity was 12, which is consistent with reported data for Black men.

Two of the young men still dated the mothers of their children; they all maintained regular contact with their children. The male group met once a week for 8 weeks in l-hour sessions during the school day and took one 3-hour field trip on a teacher workday. The meetings were scheduled on a rotating basis so that group members did not miss the same class more than twice. They were required to obtain assignments ahead of time and to keep up in their course work.

Incorporating Family Work into Individual Counselling

The counselling relationship accounts for fully thirty percent of client progress. In *Family Counselling for all Counsellors*, Kaplan posits that achieving a positive relationship with a client's family can be difficult. Family members often initially challenge the counselor's authority due to protectiveness and embarrassment. People tend to be much more protective of their families than they are of themselves, and they do not like to admit that a stranger is needed to handle family problems. It is the counselor's responsibility to establish a therapeutic relationship under these circumstances.

When the counselor is able to successfully navigate this initial stage, the therapeutic nature of the counselling relationship is enhanced for both the presenting client and the familial unit. Conversely, a family that remains distrustful of the counselor will not allow progress to occur. There are two pivotal areas the counselor and client must address upon deciding to involve a family in the client's counselling sessions: how to get the family to come into the office, and how to conduct the first session so as to increase the likelihood that subsequent sessions will occur when necessary.

There are several practical steps a counselor should take to facilitate the establishment of a positive therapeutic relationship with families. These steps include: displaying professional credentials, dressing appropriately for the session, providing a comfortable seating arrangement, and obtaining informed consent. Establishing rapport and a relationship with clients is only the first step in counselling, but it is one that sets the tone for the therapeutic experience.

Family counselling work is qualitatively different from individual counselling. Due to both the number of individuals in the room and the nature of their relationship, it is important that the counselor be prepared for new and complex dynamics. The counselor should begin the first session by making an opening statement about why the family is there. This allows the counselor to set the tone for a positive, strength-based approach.

It can be simply stated that everyone is gathered together because the counselor needs the family's help to deal with a problem. In addition, it can be stated that the gathered family members have valuable resources, background information, and ideas that will make the counselling much more efficient and effective than if the client were worked with individually. Family members may feel more relaxed when they begin to realise that the counselor is not out to blame the family for the presenting problem.

Kaplan presents several typical familial roles that a counselor can spot and utilise therapeutically. The family scapegoat, for example, might become obvious as soon as the family has arranged their seating. Families will sometimes choose a member to blame as the source of all or most family disturbances. A counselor can often tell when the client is the family scapegoat because other family members will cluster around each other and leave the client alone in a different part of the room. It is as if they are pointing and saying, "It is all his/her fault. This family would be fine if they wouldn't keep screwing up."

This person is frequently the presenting client. When visually noting that the family has isolated a family member it may be helpful to ask, "If we could wave a magic wand and everything was okay with [fill in client's name], would everything be all right with the family? Or would there still be problems?" This type of inquiry can help the family begin to address complex familial relationships, the ways in which current perceptions of one another are based in past experiences, and how families can build healthier relationships for the future.

A second role the counselor might identify in the first session is that of the gatekeeper. The gatekeeper guards the safety of the family in the counselling office. Gatekeepers can often be detected through seating arrangements as well as they will typically seat themselves between the counselor and the family. The gatekeeper will determine whether this is a safe environment for the family. The gatekeeper will control whether family members speak openly and will also be the one who decides if the family returns for future sessions. Ultimately, the gatekeeper can control the way in which the counselor can or cannot establish a relationship with the family.

Credentials

The counselor's relationship with the family begins in the counselor's reception area. When a family is waiting for a session to begin, they should be able to view the counselor's graduate diploma(s), license and professional certifications. It is also useful to have a one-page waiting room resume that states the counselor's qualifications and strengths. This resume should include a listing of credentials, experience, professional affiliations, publications, and presentations. Providing this information in the waiting room allows the counselor to begin to establish credibility (and therefore trust) with a family even before they enter the office for the first time.

Dress

There are some topics that warrant revisiting no matter how long one has been a counselor. Appropriate attire for a family counselling session is such a topic. It is recommended that the counselor dress formally (e.g., a suit) when working with families. Formal attire serves two subtle purposes during the initial stages of family counselling: it is a sign of the counselor's respect for the family, and it gives the message that the counselor is an expert. Establishing expertise is a critical component in establishing a positive therapeutic relationship with a family.

Seating

It is useful to have flexible seating in the office for conducting family work. Movable chairs mixed in with a loveseat, for example, allow family members to adjust personal space to their comfort. It also provides the counselor with insight into family dynamics, i.e., nonverbal messages, alliances, and roles. An office that is comfortable for individual counselling yet can also accommodate a family of five will take care of most seating needs. It is useful to have additional high-quality, padded folding chairs available for large family groups. Groups of larger than seven oreight relatives may be facilitated by seating arrangements appropriate to a group counselling session and may require a biggerroom.

Informed Consent

Informed consent refers to the provision of information about a counselor's practice to a family so that they can make a knowledgeable decision about whether to enter into a counselling relationship. It covers issues such as confidentiality, the counselor's treatment approach and educational background, as well as information relating to fees and making appointments. Taking time during the first family counselling session to review a handout on informed consent helps establish a positive therapeutic relationship because it promotes trust. A family that understands the purpose and limits of the family counselling session is more likely to invest in a partnership with a counselor.

Family Caregiving

Individuals in their sixties or seventies may find themselves being the primary caregivers for parents or other relatives in their eighties and nineties. The increase in childlessness and the trend toward having fewer children will result in fewer adult children to care for a greater number of older adults in the future. The trend toward more women being employed leaves these traditional caregivers little time to care for an elderly relative in addition to other responsibilities. The increased divorce rate and the geographic mobility and dispersion of families will also make it difficult for families to provide the care needed by the elderly.

Although anyone can become a caregiver, caregivers tend to be women who are approximately 57 years old. Adult children caring for a parent tend to be between 40 and 59 years old. Most are married women with families of their own. An estimated 44% of caregiving daughters and 55% of caregiving sons are employed. These statistics suggest that many adult children caring for their parents have family and work obligations that may conflict with caregiving responsibilities.

Caregiving spouses tend to be in their late 60s and 70s. When compared to the general population, caregivers are less likely to be employed and more likely to be poor or near poor and in fair to poor health. The majority of caregivers have been providing care for 1-4 years; 80% of family caregivers provide unpaid assistance seven days a week and primary caregivers report spending between four and six hours a day in caregiving duties.

Distinctions are often made between objective and subjective caregiver burden or between caregiver burden and stress, with objective burden referring to management of tasks to be performed and subjective burden or stress referring to the appraisal of the strain on the caregiver. Both burden and stress must be examined to assess the effects of caregiving on the caregiver. Caregiving is a time-consuming responsibility which inflicts various limitations on the caregiver's personal life. Confinement has been cited as the most stressful infringement on the caregiver's lifestyle.

Restriction of one's social life is the most frequently cited problem among caregivers of moderately and severely impaired persons. Role conflict resulting from the competing demands of the care recipient, other family obligations, and employment responsibilities is often a major complaint of caregivers. In addition to competing roles, many caregivers must adjust to a new role. Becoming a caregiver results in a change in the former relationship between the caregiver and the care recipient.

Seventy-seven percent of employed women who also provide care reported experiencing a conflict between work and caregiving demands, and 35% believed that being a caregiver adversely affected their work. The emotional and physical demands of the care recipient can also cause stress among caregivers. Caregivers experience more stress if the care recipient's impairment results in disruptive behaviour and improper social functioning. Several studies have shown that the degree of caregiver stress increases as the care recipient's level of functional impairment becomes more severe.

Many caregivers experience problems with the physical demands of caregiving. Caregiving spouses reported grief over the loss of the spouse they once knew. Seventy-six percent reported worrying about their own health and what would happen if they became ill. Many expressed some form of generalised anxiety about the future. Sixty-seven percent reported feeling depressed. Many caregivers report family conflict and the loss of friends and activities as a result of caregiving. The emotional and physical strains of caregiving often lead to deterioration in the caregiver's own health. Although caregivers report physical, financial, and family strains associated with caregiving, the most negative consequences of caregiving on caregivers seem to be the emotional strain of caregiver burdens.

Common Coping Response

The most common coping response of the caregiving spouses studied by Barusch was to seek help when they had problems, especially in the areas of care management and health problems. The second most common coping response was to simply not cope. Spouses reported not coping with sexual problems, guilt feelings, feeling their spouse was overly dependent, arguments with their spouse, excessive demands made by others, worries about future financial problems, managing money, and worries about their own health. Another study found that 12% of caregivers drank alcohol to cope with the psychological strains of caregiving.

Effective Coping Strategies

Interventions designed to help caregivers cope with caregiver burden and stress have focused on individual coping strategies, respite services, and support groups and other group interventions. Results from studies evaluating the effectiveness of different interventions have been equivocal.

Individual Coping Strategies. Caregivers themselves report having the most success when they could somehow change a stressful situation and reported highest levels of satisfaction when they could change it alone.

Respite Care. Compared with caregivers receiving no respite care, caregivers of Alsheimer's patients who had formal respite care were able to keep their relatives out of institutions for a longer time. Participants reported high levels of satisfaction with respite services, yet respite neither alleviated caregiver burden nor promoted caregiver mental health significantly. A programme which provided adult day care services to older adults with dementia did report a reduction of caregiver burden.

Group Interventions. One study of a group intervention for family caregivers of dementia patients showed that, at post-treatment, caregivers who received the intervention showed no greater change in caregiver depression, life satisfaction, coping, or social activity than did caregivers on a waiting list who received no intervention.

In one study, individuals caring for impaired elderly relatives were assigned to either a waiting-list control group or to one of five treatment groups that received different combinations of services, including seminars for caregivers, support groups, family consultation services, and respite care. One interesting finding from this study was the reluctance of participants to use services. In spite of free access to services and encouragement to use services, almost one-third of caregivers did not use services.

Challenges to Caregiving Responsibilities

The reluctance of family caregivers to use services for which they are eligible and the preference of caregivers to solve problems on their own present challenges to those trying to provide services to family caregivers. Caregivers who have little time to meet their family, work, and caregiving responsibilities often feel they do not have any time left for support groups or other interventions. Simply locating family caregivers in need of support and getting them to accept such support may prove difficult. Many family caregivers do not seek outside help until they have reached a crisis point.

Barusch recommends that training programmes teach techniques for personal control in order to help caregivers cope without outside help, but also provide information about community resources and discuss caregiver feelings about seeking and accepting help in an effort to prepare the caregivers for a time when they may be unable to cope alone.

Counselling for Eating Disorders

Bulimia and Anorexia

Bulimia and anorexia are binge-eating and starving disorders afflicting thousands of adolescent and young adult women each year.

The majority of bulimics binge in secret and resort to self-induced vomiting or purging. A typical binge averages 4,000 calories, lasts an hour, and occurs twice a day. Diagnostic criteria include recurrent episodes of binge-eating; awareness that the eating pattern is abnormal and fear of being unable to stop voluntarily; and depressed mood and self-deprecating thoughts after binging.

Anorexics may also binge/purge and abuse physical exercise. Usually, they suffer from more severe psychological and medical problems than bulimics. Diagnostic criteria include a 25% weight loss or a body weight 25% below normal; an intense fear of becoming obese that does not diminish with weight loss; a distorted body image (feeling fat or "just right" even when emaciated); and a refusal to maintain weight above a minimum norm for age and height.

Bulimics and anorexics typically come from families who depend excessively on each other and cannnot handle stess and anger. "Enmeshed" is an apt description: what they consume, wear and do and how well they appear, behave, and perform are all regarded as everybody's business and extremely important. Paradoxically, the eating disorder functions to preserve family stability. The victim secures some sense of identity, approval, and control through the special attention her illness requires; other members acquire a unifying focus for their own roles. The net effect is to reinforce the family's mutual dependencies and to hide underlying conflicts.

Counselling Programmes

Multidisciplinary intervention programmes offering individual and family or group counselling, as well as adjunct self-help or support groups, are able to help significant numbers of the eating disordered. The most successful programme combines individual with family counselling and uses a team approach that includes a physician and nutritionist. Chemical dependency programmes often provide useful models. The core elements of the three types of counselling programmes are individual counselling, family counselling, and group counselling.

Individual counselling

Individual counselling involves journal keeping; nutritional intervention; altering antecedent events; using cognitive-behavioural techniques; manipulating consequences; and eliciting the support of family and friends.

Family counselling

Family counselling involves discussing realistically how the disorder affects each member; designing tasks to fit the developmental level of each member; providing alternate ways to respond to the illness; establishing rules of eating conduct to clarify areas of control and responsibility; helping members meet each others' emotional needs; and looking for abusive or addictive patterns in other members.

Group counselling

Group couseling involves educating the group on family dynamics, dependency, stress management, nutrition, womens' issues, depression, feelings, sexuality and assertiveness; using a mix of therapeutic devices, such as rational-emotive techniques, gestalt and process techniques, spiritual counselling, neurolinguistic programmeming, behaviour modification, desensitisation and confrontation.

Among client populations of bulimics, 63% to 80% eventually become binge/purge-free; among anorexics, 50% regain normal weight and eating habits, 25% improve but have pronounced weight and/or eating habit problems, and 25% are resistent to intervention. Early identification and treatment are crucial to a successful outcome for both disorders.

PARENTS' GUIDE TO GIFTED CHILDREN

Giftedness is 'asynchronous development' in which advanced cognitive abilities and heightened intensity combine to create inner experiences and awareness that are qualitatively different from the norm. This asynchrony increases with higher intellectual capacity. The uniqueness of the gifted renders them particularly vulnerable and requires modifications in parenting, teaching and counselling in order for them to develop optimally.

"Asynchrony" means being out of sync, both internally and externally. "Asynchronous development" means that gifted children develop cognitively at a much faster rate than they develop physically and emotionally, posing some interesting problems. For example, ideas forged by 8-year-old minds may be difficult to produce with 5-year-old hands. Further, advanced cognition often makes gifted children aware of information that they are not yet emotionally ready to handle. They tend to experience all of life with greater intensity, rendering them emotionally complex.

These children usually do not fit the developmental norms for their age; they have more advanced play interests and often are academically far ahead of their age peers. The brighter the child, the greater the asynchrony and potential vulnerability. Therefore, parents who are aware of the inherent developmental differences of their children can prepare themselves to act as their advocates.

Some of the earliest signs of giftedness include:

— unusual alertness in infancy

— less need for sleep in infancy

— long attention span

— high activity level

— smiling or recognising caretakers early

— intense reactions to noise, pain, frustration

— advanced progression through the developmental milestones

— extraordinary memory

— enjoyment and speed of learning

— early and extensive language development

— fascination with books

— curiosity

— excellent sense of humor

— abstract reasoning and problem-solving skills

— vivid imagination (e.g., imaginary companions)
— sensitivity and compassion

If a child exhibits a majority of these characteristics, parents may wish to have the child assessed by an experienced examiner to find out if the child is gifted. Firstborn children tend to be recognised more often than their siblings. When one child in the family is gifted, it is quite possible that others may also be gifted. Early identification is recommended (ages 3 through 8) because it permits early intervention, as important for gifted as for any other children with special needs.

Receptive Parenting

Children learn first from their parents. Parents who spend time with their gifted child are more able to tune in to their child's interests and respond by offering appropriate educational enrichment opportunities. It is important that parents read to their children frequently, even when the children are capable of reading to themselves. In the early years, parents can help their children discover their personal interests, expose their children to their own interests, and encourage their children to learn about a wide variety of subjects such as art, nature, music, museums, and sports. Children who are attracted to a particular area need opportunities to explore that field in depth. Home stimulation and support of interests is vital to the development of talents. Following the lead of the child will help the child flourish.

Gifted children often can exhaust and overwhelm a new mother and father. Gifted infants often sleep less than other babies and require extra stimulation when they are awake. It is helpful to have extended family in the home, grandparents who live nearby, a close community of friends or relatives, or a teenager in the neighborhood who can spend some time with the child so that the primary caretakers can get some rest to do other things. For single parents, such support is particularly important. From the time they can talk, gifted children are constantly asking questions and often challenge authority. "Do it because I said so" doesn't work with these children. Generally, parents who take the time to explain requests get more cooperation than do more authoritarian parents. If these children are spoken to and listened to with consideration and respect, they tend to respond respectfully.

As children get older, a family meeting can be a good way of sharing responsibility and learning negotiation skills. Family meetings can provide a forum where children have a voice as a family member, and provide avenues for avoiding power struggles that otherwise can occur. It is important for gifted children to feel emotionally supported by the family—even when there are disagreements.

School Placement

Gifted children generally benefit by spending at least some time in the classroom with children of similar abilities. Their educational programme should be designed to foster progress at their own rate of development. Parents who become involved with the school can help administrators and teachers be responsive to the needs of these children.

Open, flexible environments provide students with opportunities for choices, and enhance independence and creativity. Early entrance or other forms of acceleration may be considered when the school gifted programme is not sufficiently challenging or when there is no opportunity for gifted children to be grouped with age peers who are intellectually advanced.

Early entrance is the easiest form of acceleration, academically and socially. It may be best to accelerate girls before third grade or after ninth grade, when they are less bonded to their peer group. Boys are usually more willing to skip grades at any point in their school programme. Excellent guidelines for acceleration are provided by Feldhusen. When a child expresses a willingness to be accelerated, the chances are good that an excellent social adjustment will be made. In the preschool and primary years, mixed-aged groupings are beneficial, as long as the gifted child is not the oldest in the group.

Advocacy of Parents

Gifted children need strong, responsible advocates, and parent groups can make a difference. It takes persistence of large groups of parents to assure that provisions for gifted children are kept firmly in place. Parents of children who are gifted need opportunities to share parenting experiences with each other, and parent groups can provide a place where that can happen. It is important for parents of any children with special needs to meet with the teachers early in the school year.

When parents and teachers work together, appropriate programmes can be developed and problems can be caught early. It is helpful for parents to offer to assist their child's teacher by making or locating supplemental materials, helping in the classroom or library, offering expertise to small groups of students, or finding others who can provide other enrichment experiences. Effective parents stay involved in their children's education and informed about gifted education in general. When a teacher makes a special effort to understand or assist a gifted child, a note to the teacher or to the principal is generally appreciated.

8

Collaborative Group Guidance and Counselling

Collaboration in Family Literacy Education

Policymakers, attracted by the logic of inclusive, family-oriented services, have legislated collaboration into various programmes for children and their families. How is collaboration different from traditional service delivery for language minority adults, in which one agency provides the language instruction, another provides job placement, and another provides counselling services? Is there collaboration whenever two or more agencies share information for and about clients and refer the clients to other agencies for needed services?

The following are the distinctions among cooperation, coordination, and collaboration.

1. *Cooperation*—Each group retains its own authority and keeps its own resources. Cooperation can take place among groups with differing goals and without a clearly defined shared mission. There is little risk in this relationship and little gain, as there is no real sharing of goods, services, and expertise.

2. *Coordination*—Each group retains its individual authority and independence, but specific modifications in the way it operates may begin to occur. Coordination requires mutual planning and open communication among groups as mission and goals begin to be shared. Partners enjoy the benefits of shared resources, yet power may become an issue among participating groups.
3. *Collaboration*—Separate groups with commitment to a common mission come together to form a new structure. Collaboration requires comprehensive planning as decision-making, power, authority, and resources are shared. These synergistic efforts often result in innovations that benefit all participants: clients, service providers, and the wider community. In true collaboration, partners no longer run parallel programmes at a common site, but have created a new programme that offers participants more than the individual agencies can offer separately.

Collaboration Framework

Although research indicates that there is no one way to collaborate, resource books share successful strategies, provide guidelines and suggestions, illustrate with examples, and warn of potential barriers or predictable pitfalls. One framework helps potential partners to think about the collaborative process as a series of changes in interactions among individuals and the organisations they represent, rather than as a set of sequential steps.

1. "Envision Results by Working Individual-to-Individual" Individuals representing the collaborating groups meet to confirm their shared vision and specify desired results.

2. "Empower Oneself by Working Individual-to-Organisation" Clear authority provided by both the home organisation and the collaboration empowers individuals to act. This process entails confirming organisational roles, resolving conflicts, organising efforts, and supporting members.

3. "Ensure Success by Working Organisation-to-Organisation" Envisioned services are provided and articulated goals are realised as the collaborative learns to manage the work, create joint systems, evaluate the results, and renew its efforts toward achieving desired results.

4. "Equip for Continuity by Working Collaboration-to-Community" The completion of the original collaboration often becomes the genesis of a new, more comprehensive collaboration as collaborators establish continuity for their successes by extending their relationships and responsibilities to include the broader community.

Use of new technologies

Technology is making collaboration possible beyond the physical limits of traditional work environments and geographical locations. Teleconferencing facilitates information sharing by enabling individuals to communicate across the boundaries of time and space by telephone, television, or computer. Technologies are now available to take educators beyond teleconferencing by providing online forums for interactive meetings anywhere in the world. State-of-the-art collaboration technology is exemplified by Xerox's LiveBoard, an electronic blackboard that utilises computer video technology. LiveBoard operates via ordinary phone lines and allows collaborators in single or multiple locations to share a common writing and viewing surface for capturing ideas; organising information; and viewing, editing, and annotating documents.

Ethical aspects

Ethical questions arise in collaboration. Since collaboration involves shared power and decision-making, what ethical basis will individuals representing diverse groups use to make decisions? How will individual rights and group interests be preserved in the face of new organisational structures? Griesel offers collaborators a series of tools (including checklists, paradigms, and more sophisticated models) for use in examining ethical considerations. Her ten-point ethical guidelines for collaboration include questions about personal, professional, and public responsibility.

Evaluating collaboration

Methods for evaluating collaboration are being developed. Most of these focus on process variables to help collaborators gauge their progress. A fundamental question for any partnership assessing its effort is, "Does our work meet the 'shared decision-making' criterion for true collaboration?" Schlessman-Frost and Saunders have developed a model to organise and clarify information to answer that fundamental question. This model provides a framework for determining the degree of collaboration in a partnership by classifying each collaborator's contributing activities as cooperation, coordination, and collaboration.

Policy implications

Trends toward collaboration raise policy and advocacy

issues within adult ESL education. Funding agencies' definitions of family could contain subtle (or more blatant) biases. If a family must include children in order to qualify for services, the inclusive intent of integrated, comprehensive services may be contradicted, as childless adults are denied access to these services. A collaborative group might address such a policy issue in two ways. First, the group could work with the community, the collaborating partners, and potential participants to coordinate advocacy efforts for policy changes. Second, instead of waiting for the rules to change, the existing collaborative group could use its effective intra- or inter-organisational structure to combine resources in innovative ways to make services available for those who might be excluded.

Collaboration at the state level among ABE programmes, including special education, bilingual and ESL education, and alternative secondary and GED instruction, could produce innovative services to meet the diverse needs of adults. Perhaps advocacy for mandated collaboration for ESL literacy in the Vocational and Adult Education Acts and in other legislation which provides instructional and social services to adults is worth considering.

Guidance and Counselling for Dropout Intervention

High dropout rates among students from economically disadvantaged and non-English-speaking backgrounds are among the major concerns of middle and high school educators in the United States. Though dropout rates have declined overall in recent years, especially among Blacks and Whites, the trend for Hispanic students is quite the opposite.

Middle and high school students are paired as tutors with elementary school students identified as being at risk of dropping out of school. Tutors are paid minimum wage for their work. The programme's philosophy is that the tutors, by being placed in paid positions of responsibility and treated as adults, will improve their self-esteem and academic performance. As one tutor claimed, "When I'm helping these kids, I'm helping myself. I'm learning things when I'm tutoring them". In turn, the student being tutored will grow both academically and personally under the attention of the tutor and will be encouraged to remain in school until graduation.

Cross-age tutoring, the main component of the VYP, takes place at the elementary school one hour a day, four days a week; on the fifth day, the tutors take a class on effective tutoring strategies. In addition to conducting the tutoring sessions, tutors must adhere to the employee guidelines of their host school and report to a teacher coordinator, who monitors and evaluates their progress. Student tutors also attend classes in English as a second language and content areas.

Field trips, conducted at least twice a year, are designed to broaden students' horizons by exposing them to cultural and professional possibilities in their communities. A student recognition component serves to instill a sense of self-worth in both tutors and tutees. This takes the form of a celebratory lunch or dinner, media attention, or presentation of merit awards for student efforts to stay in school and help others do the same. Finally, adults who are successful in their field, have the same language and cultural background as the students, and have overcome similar obstacles act as role models and provide guidance to both the tutors and the tutees.

BIBLIOTHERAPY

Bibliotherapy is a family of technique for structuring interaction between a facilitator and a participant based on mutual sharing of literature. The idea of healing through books is not a new one—it can be traced far back in history, from the days of the first libraries in Greece. The use of books in healing, however, has been interpreted differently by classical scholars, physicians, psychologists, social workers, nurses, parents, teachers, librarians, and counsellors. There is, in fact, confusion in determining the dividing line between reading guidance and bibliotherapy.

Bibliotherapy generally appears to be more successful as an adjunctive therapy. Despite such mixed research results, however, interest in the use of bibliotherapy appears to have increased in the past few years. This most likely reflects the increase of societal and familial problems in the United States—rise in divorce, alienation of young people, excessive peer group pressure, alcohol and drug abuse, and so on. Educators have also begun to recognise the increasingly critical need for delivering literacy instruction to at-risk and homeless children and their families.

Bibliotherapeutic intervention may be undertaken for many reasons:

1) to develop an individual's self-concept;
2) to increase an individual's understanding of human behaviour or motivations;
3) to foster an individual's honest self-appraisal;
4) to provide a way for a person to find interests outside of self;
5) to relieve emotional or mental pressure;

6) to show an individual that he or she is not the first or only person to encounter such a problem;

7) to show an individual that there is more than one solution to a problem;

(8) to help a person discuss a problem more freely; and

9) to help an individual plan a constructive course of action to solve a problem.

Before undertaking bibliotherapy, however, a practitioner must remember that it is more than just the casual recommendation of a certain book to an individual—it is a deliberate course of action that requires careful planning.

Whether you are a classroom teacher, a librarian, or a mental health professional, be advised that bibliotherapy must be handled with great delicacy, and not every practitioner possesses the personal qualifications to be a facilitator in the process. Those who are interested, however, should possess personal stability; a genuine interest in working with others; and the ability to empathise with others without moralising, threatening, or commanding.

In addition, Smith recommends working with another practitioner or authority in a different field. For example, if you are a language arts teacher, you might collaborate with the school librarian, a guidance counselor, or the school psychologist. This cooperation helps in balancing the process so that no one person is "in charge." Smith also feels that facilitators need to have a light-enough tone in discussing problems so that no one becomes upset, but a thoughtful-enough manner to allow for "comfortable discussion." She also feels that fictional works are best for discussion purposes because participants can talk about the characters in a book rather than about themselves.

All parties must agree to the bibliotherapy, however. A recent study on generating reading interest in adolescents with handicaps found that the majority were not even interested in reading novels with handicapped characters. Most of the young people in the survey "seemed to view the term 'handicapped' in a very narrow sense and reject the word and anything to which it may be connected."

A practitioner must also decide whether an individual or a group therapy approach would be best in the particular situation. Individual therapy requires time-consuming one-on-one sessions, but some people feel freer to express themselves in a one-on-one situation. For a classroom teacher, of course, the classroom could be seen as a natural group, and it would be a group easily broken up into collaborative units.

According to Pardeck and Pardeck, groups can be a powerful vehicle for helping to heal emotional problems. The Pardecks believe that a group approach to learning enhances the total child. The group approach allows members to share common experiences, thus lessening anxieties. It can create a feeling of belonging and can also provide security for individuals who might feel uncomfortable in situations where they are singled out for special attention. Working in a group may lead an individual to develop a different perspective and a new understanding of the problems of others.

Regardless of whether the practitioner chooses the individual or group approach, the basic procedures in conducting bibliotherapy are:

1) motivate the individual or individuals with introductory activities;
2) provide time for reading the material;

3) allow incubation time;
4) provide follow-up discussion time, using questions that will lead persons from literal recall of information through interpretation, application, analysis, synthesis, and evaluation of that information; and
5) conduct evaluation and direct the individual or individuals toward closure—this involves both evaluation by the practitioner and self-evaluation by the individual.

Identification, Intervention and Prevention of Teenage Suicide

Adolescence is a time when ordinary levels of stress are heightened by physical, psychological, emotional, and social changes. Adolescents suffer a feeling of loss for the childhood they must leave behind, and undergo an arduous period of adjustment to their new adult identity. In single-parent families, this adjustment may be even more difficult. Yet society alienates adolescents from their new identity by not allowing them the rights and responsibilities of adulthood. They are no longer children, but they are not accorded the adult privileges of expressing their sexuality or holding a place in the work force.

There is increased pressure to stay in school, where success is narrowly defined and difficult to achieve. In an affluent society which emphasises immediate rewards, adolescents are not taught to be tolerant of frustration. Blurred gender roles can also be confusing and frustrating for teens.

Some researchers attribute teenage suicide to the weakening of the family unit. They argue that economic and political institutions have penetrated it, reducing it to a consumer unit no longer able to function as a support system, and no longer able to supply family members with a sense of stability and rootedness. Awareness of the existing state of the world, now threatened by sophisticated methods of destruction, can cause depression which contributes to the adolescent's sense of frustration, helplessness, and hopelessness. Faced with these feelings and lacking coping mechanisms, adolescents can become overwhelmed and turn to escapist measures such as drugs, withdrawal, and ultimately suicide.

Process of Identification

Contrary to popular belief, suicide is not an impulsive act but the result of a three-step process: a previous history of problems is compounded by problems associated with adolescence; finally, a precipitating event, often a death or the end of a meaningful relationship, triggers the suicide. Long-term problems can include: losing a parent or close relative at a young age; coming from a family of divorce, or one in which there is much discord; being a victim of domestic violence or child abuse; or living with an alcoholic in the family.

Hyperactivity or undiagnosed learning disabilities also pose serious long-term problems for adolescents. These problems can create further difficulties for the adolescent, causing social isolation and withdrawal, poor school performance and attendance, and repeated suicide attempts. The precipitating event which triggers a suicide attempt is usually a family crisis, a significant personal loss, or an upset to self-esteem (such as failing a course, losing one's place on a sports team or being fired from a part-time job). The anniversary of a loss can also evoke a powerful desire to commit suicide.

Warning signs

Many behavioural and verbal clues—some subtle, others more obvious—can alert the informed parent, teacher, counselor or friend to an adolescent's suicidal intentions. A teen at risk of committing suicide is experiencing deep depression, which may be indicated by loss of weight, appetite or interest in personal appearance; a change in sleeping pattern; fatigue; and feelings of hopelessness and low self-esteem. Sudden behavioural changes may occur: the youth may become disruptive, violent, or hostile toward family and friends; or unexplainably moody, suspicious, anxious, or selfish. He or she may spend a great deal of time daydreaming, fantasising, or imagining ills, in extreme cases experiencing memory lapses or hallucinations.

Some signals should come through loud and clear: the teenager may express a desire to die, threaten to commit suicide, or inform friends of a plan. Self-abusive acts such as cutting off hair and self-inflicting cigarette burns are obvious suicidal gestures. The teen may develop a preoccupation with death and dying, make arrangements to give away prised possessions, withdraw from therapeutic help, or rapidly lose interest in once-valued activities and objects.

Psychological first aid

Most youths who attempt suicide don't really want to die; they are crying out for help. There seems to be universal agreement on the manner in which to counsel suicidal teens:

1. Be non-judgmental.
2. Treat the youth's problems seriously, and take all threats seriously.

3. Do not try to talk the person out of it.
4. Ask direct questions, such as, "Have you been thinking of killing yourself?" Don't be afraid that you will be suggesting something the adolescent has not yet considered; usually your mentioning the topic is a relief.
5. Communicate your concern and support.
6. Offer yourself as a caring listener until professional help can be arranged.
7. Try to evaluate the seriousness of the risk, in order to make the appropriate referral to a health care professional, counselor, or concerned teacher.
8. Do not swear to secrecy. Contact someone who can help the adolescent if he or she will not do it personally.
9. Do not leave the person alone if you feel the threat is immediate.

In a counselling situation, a contract can be an effective prevention technique. The adolescent signs a card which states that he or she agrees not to take the final step of suicide while interacting with the counselor. Once past the crisis, follow-up is crucial, because most suicides occur within three months of the beginning of improvement, when the youth has the energy to carry out plans conceived earlier. Regularly scheduled supportive counselling should be provided to teach the youth coping mechanisms for managing stress accompanying a life crisis, as well as day-to-day stress.

Prevention methods

Community members, mental health professionals, school

personnel, peers, and parents can play major roles in the prevention of teenage suicide. Programmes that build adolescents' self-esteem and inspire a sense of inclusion in society rather than alienation from it have been found to be particularly effective.

Churches and other religious communities can sponsor suicide prevention programmes, and engage youth in the planning and implementation of programmes for aiding the elderly, working in day care centers, training peer counsellors, and improving the environment. Libraries can sponsor similar programmes which teens can develop, manage, and supervise themselves.

Afterschool programmes can be established in community centers to provide organised outings for cultural enrichment, computer training, tutoring, job counselling, sexuality counselling, crisis intervention, and/or health care. When staffed by people who care, these centers have the potential to become solid support networks for teenagers.

Mental health personnel can educate students, counsellors, teachers, and others, such as nurses and religious youth group leaders, in suicide identification and prevention. They can lead crisis intervention workshops for counsellors and teachers and train peer counsellors in middle and high schools. They can establish suicide crisis centers with telephone hotlines, support groups, outreach teams to facilitate grief groups for families and in schools, and research facilities for further study.

School counsellors can act as liaisons between the community and the school, between mental health professionals and teachers, and between suicidal teens and parents. They can also:

Alert school officials to the seriousness of the issue—Sponsor staff development workshops to alert teachers to potential suicide risks—Present educational films to the school population—Offer stress management workshops to teens —Train peer counsellors—Establish support groups for teens—Staff drop-in centers, providing a counselling atmosphere of support and acceptance —Construct a referral network of psychiatrists, psychologists, and social workers to contact in case of emergency—Arrange remedial reading courses to alleviate feelings of frustration and low self-esteem in adolescents with reading problems—Advocate that the school offer a wide variety of extracurricular activities to youth —Encourage more personalised teacher-student relationships

Teachers play an especially important part in prevention, because they spend so much time with their students. Along with holding parent-teacher meetings to discuss teenage suicide prevention, teachers can form referral networks with mental health professionals. They can increase student awareness by introducing the topic in health classes. Students should learn how to identify those at risk of suicide, how to intervene with good listening and communication skills, and where to turn for help.

Peers are crucial to suicide prevention. According to one survey, 93% of the students reported that they would turn to a friend before a teacher, parent or spiritual guide in a time of crisis. Peers can form student support groups and, once educated themselves, can train others to be peer counsellors.

Finally, parents need to be as open and as attentive as possible to their adolescent children's difficulties. The most effective suicide prevention technique parents can exercise is to maintain open lines of communication with their

children. Sometimes teens hide their problems, not wanting to burden the people they love. It is extremely important to assure teens that they can share their troubles, and gain support in the process.

Parents are encouraged to talk about suicide with their children, and to educate themselves by forming study groups with other parents, or by attending parent-teacher or parent-counselor education sessions. Once trained, parents can help to staff a crisis hotline in their community. Parents also need to be involved in the counselling process if a teen has suicidal tendencies. These activities may both alleviate parents' fears of the unknown and assure teenagers that their parents care.

It is possible, through the coordinated actions of parents, peers, school personnel, and the community at large, to reverse the growing trend of teenage suicide. Counsellors can make the difference, by providing the leadership and motivation to guide the efforts of youngsters and adults.

Filial Therapy

ilial therapy is an alternative method for treating emotionally disturbed children in which the parent is used as an ally in the therapeutic process. The parent becomes the child's primary therapeutic agent. Parental involvement in a child's developmental process facilitates the parent's motivation to continue sessions and thus tends to eliminate the typical parental resistance that is encountered when the parent is not involved in the child's therapy.

Guerney reported the primary source of maladjustment, for many children living with their families, could logically be traced to interpersonal relationships within the family. Filial therapy teaches the parent a new way of interacting with their child, thus improving the parent-child relationship. Additionally, filial therapy provides focused attention to the child from a person who holds emotional significance to the child, thus encouraging anxieties learned by the parental influence to be unlearned, and provides opportunities for miscommunications to be clarified to the child by the parent.

This approach is based on the therapeutic nature of play and the parent's ability to learn to assume the therapeutic role required of them for a short period of time under special conditions. The parent's new role permits a child to explore personal struggles by breaking previous patterns of parent-child interaction. It also is expected that parents will generalise new patterns to life outside of the play sessions.

Process of Filial Therapy

Filial Therapy is an approach used by play therapists to train parents to be therapeutic agents with their own children. Parents are taught basic child-centered play therapy principles and skills, including reflective listening, recognising and responding to children's feelings, therapeutic limit setting, building children's self-esteem, and structuring required weekly play sessions with their children using selected toys. The therapist typically utilises didactic instruction, demonstration play sessions, role-playing, group discussion, required at-home laboratory play sessions, videotapes, and supervision in a supportive atmosphere to educate parents. Parents learn how to create a warm, nonjudgmental, unconditionally accepting, genuine, and understanding environment in which their child feels safe to explore the parent-child relationship and themselves, including fears, desires, feelings, and struggles.

After a parent passes an initial screening to ensure the parent and child are appropriate candidates, the parent is placed in a parenting training group, composed of six to eight parents of children ages three to ten, that can include mothers, fathers, and spouses from other families. The parents are given opportunities to express their parenting and play session concerns and struggles with the group at weekly meetings. As the therapist deems necessary, filial therapy training groups last six to eighteen months.

Initial training's are spent exploring the parent child relationship and establishing a commitment from the parents. The parent's role is modeled after that of a child-centered play therapist. Training emphasises skills such as reflection of feeling, tracking, limit setting, and increasing parental sensitivity to their children. Once an adequate skill level is met, parents begin in home play sessions with their child. Parents are given a defined therapeutic role to play for a defined period of time and provided with feedback and supervision by the therapist and fellow parents in the following weekly training group.

During assigned play sessions, the parent is expected to be empathic, understanding and accepting, while allowing the child to direct the play. It is critical that the parent be able to convey this understanding and acceptance to their child. These conditions facilitate both the child's expression of emotion and a new perceptual awareness from the parent about their child. When children are permitted to express themselves without losing status in the eyes of their parents the children's anxiety diminishes. The child feels validated and valued, and is able to master difficulties and feelings rather than try to distort and deny them. As these changes occur and the child experiences the parent in a new manner, the child begins to understand his or her sense of worth.

The parent learns to set limits on the child's behaviour when needed. In order to ensure continued empathic understanding felt and conveyed by the parent, behaviour is not permitted that results in the parent or child being physically harmed. While maintaining acceptance of the child's feelings and desires, the parent learns to facilitate the child's expression in socially appropriate manners rather than overt, disruptive, harmful means.

The consistency of the special playtime, the toys used, and the relationship between parent and child results in a change in perception of the parent by the child. As the parents continue weekly at home play sessions they also attend supportive filial group meetings that explore techniques, the meaning of their child's play, and their personal emotional reactions to the sessions. The therapist meets only with the parents and works in both a didactic and in a more traditional therapeutic role with the parental group to facilitate personal exploration and skill comprehension among parents. Both the home play sessions and the group sessions make unique contributions toward helping the parent-child relationship.

The filial therapist facilitates the child's expression of a wide range of feelings by providing a wide range of toys. The playroom should communicate that all feelings are accepted. Items likely to direct a child's play, such as books or electronic toys, are avoided. The availability of items such as bop bag, dart gun, and dinosaur, conveys a message to the child that anger and aggression are accepted. Inappropriate aggressive or harmful behaviours are redirected to acceptable outlets.

Baby bottles, dolls, kitchen food and ware facilitate the expression of nurturance. A dollhouse and associated figures and furniture are often used in the expression of

family issues. The playroom should further include nondirective expressive media, such as craft and construction pieces, paint, crayons, markers, paper, clay or sand. These items encourage a variety of expression. The inclusion of a ring toss game or blocks and play money can facilitate the expression of mastery, competition, and cooperation themes.

Filial therapy is a philosophically-based process that has proven to be beneficial in a variety of settings, populations, and formats including but, not limited to: two-parent families, foster parents, single parents, incarcerated mothers, incarcerated fathers, parents of different nationalities, parents of mentally challenged children, parents of chronically ill children, parents of children demonstrating conduct problems, parents of children with learning difficulties, and non-offending parents of sexually abused children.

Originally filial therapy was developed as a long-term group approach limited to aid children age ten or younger. Since then, others have adopted the concepts and methods previously presented to intensified or individualised formats.

9

Employment Counselling

Within the current economic context of rapidly changing labour market opportunities and structural unemployment, many people are faced with the prospect of not simply losing a job, but a way of life. The loss affects the core of being and can result in a series of emotional reactions that approximate loss reactions, namely denial, anger, bargaining, depression, and acceptance. Coupled with loss is confusion of setting a new career direction and stress associated with job search. The end result can be an emotional roller coaster which is difficult for the person, the family, and for professionals trying to offer assistance.

Amundson & Borgen identified several factors that helped or hindered during unemployment. Facilitating factors included support from family and friends, positive thinking, career changes and retraining, part-time or temporary work, job search support groups, vocational counselling, initial job search activities, making job contacts, and physical activity.

Hindering factors were job rejections, financial pressures, contacts with government agencies, unknown or negative future, ineffective job search activities, negative thinking, and spouse or family problems. The hindering factors reflect the stress of job search, the re-definition of self associated with unemployment, and strained relationships. The facilitating factors focus on relationships and meaningful activities.

POTENTIAL FACTORS OF GROUP EMPLOYMENT COUNSELLING

Taken together, these factors pointed to the potential of group employment counselling. In a group context there are opportunities for support and meaningful exchange with others. In order to examine this further, investigated the experiences of people who had been involved in a variety of group employment counselling programmes. Participants were contacted 3-5 months after the groups had finished. Group employment counselling resulted in a dramatic upswing that in some cases led to a job (48 %) and in other cases to sustained, independent job search activity (52 %).

Timing of the group experience seemed particularly important. Some people tended to emotionally drift slowly downward after 2 months of being unemployed, while others maintained a positive outlook for up to 6 months, but then experienced rapid emotional decline. Participation in the group around 8-9 months after job loss seemed to produce an "emotional rebound" where people were able to maintain a more positive outlook whether or not a job was found.

When participants described their group involvement, they emphasised what they had learned, the support that they had received, and the ways in which their self-esteem had been enhanced. They appreciated the structured learning activity which was meaningful and enabled them to meet others facing similar experiences. For most people, their main regret was that they had not joined a group earlier.

Model of a Group Employment Counsel

Based on the information that task (i.e., structured learning activities) and social support aspects of groups were about equally helpful, a group employment counselling model was developed. The model has two emphases: acquisition of relevant skills and information (the "educative" element), and the development and maintenance of a constructive attitude (often impeded by emotions which must be recognised: anxiety, fear and depression).

The group counselling model focuses on the development of knowledge, skills, and personal awareness. These three elements are important regardless of the purpose of the group: career exploration, career decision-making, job search, or coping with unemployment. Within the approach, participants have the opportunity to acquire relevant information, practice skills needed to be successful, and address any barriers that they may be facing.

The model, has five core elements:

1. The "group goals and activities" define the purpose of the group.
2. "Member needs and roles" develop from two sources: (a) needs related to the career challenges of members, and (b) needs related to being a group member: inclusion, control, and trust.
3. The "group processes" influence the functioning of the group and include: communication, norm setting, decision making, confrontation of the problem, problem solving, and conflict management.

4. "Leader approaches and skills" include personal qualities necessary for group leadership, approaches (directing, influencing, assisting, and delegating) that promote effective group leadership, and particular skills (reaction, interaction, and action) necessary to respond to the needs of group members at various stages of group development.
5. "Group design" focuses on sequencing group activities to be congruent with group purpose and stage of group development.

The stages of group development provide a second dimension to the model and are consistent with Tuckman's overview of group development.

1. The "planning stage" provides a foundation for the group. Initial referral and screening are important to ensure member needs match group goals.
2. When group members first come together ("initial stage"), there is a need for members to feel part of the group (inclusion). In this stage it is important to focus on the integration of individual and group goals and the establishment of group norms.
3. As members become more aware of the needs of each other and the leader, the issue of control can become more central. This leads to a "transition stage" in which there is greater potential for reluctance and conflict.
4. Following this period of potential unrest, group members move into the "working stage," characterised by greater trust and an emphasis on commitment and productivity. The group functions with greater autonomy, and there is less reliance on the leader for support and direction.

5. As the group approaches the "termination stage" there is an opportunity to integrate what has been learned and plan for reaching goals. Emotionally, there may be feelings of loss which need to be acknowledged by the leader.

6. The "post-group" stage involves meeting after the group has finished to provide continued support and encouragement.

The model is fluid and dynamic. The five components of group development influence and are influenced by each other. They require the group leaders to be aware of group member needs and to modify activities and leadership approaches accordingly. In addition, the stages of group development do not proceed in a linear fashion. Members often return to earlier stages in their general progression through the group and leaders need to be aware of which stages group members may be in at any particular time and tailor their approach and skills accordingly.

10

Experimental Learning in Group Counselling

David Kolb proposed a model of experiential learning that describes a cycle of learning which includes concrete experience, reflective observation, abstract conceptualisation, and active experimentation. These four modes can be used to represent the ends of two continua referred to as perception (anchored by concrete experience and abstract conceptualisation) and processing (anchored by active experimentation and reflective observation). When these two dimensions are arranged as perpendicular axes, four quadrants are created that can describe learning processes and individual learning styles. When this model is applied to group counselling or other interactive learning environments, four types of experiential learning can be identified.

These learning process quadrants can be reffred as: Reflecting on Experience, Assimilating and Conceptualising, Experimenting and Practicing and Planning for Application. These learning processes will be described next and group counselling techniques that can be used to promote each type of learning will follow.

The practicality of applying Kolb's model of experiential learning to group counselling is threefold. First, this model suggests multiple group learning processes that can occur within a single session rather than focusing on broader processes that occur across the life of the group such as Yalom's therapeutic factors. Second, by suggesting different types of learning that complete a cycle of learning, this model encourages group facilitators to create comprehensive learning encounters within each group sessions that will impact members more deeply than if only one or two types of learning are emphasized. Third, by emphasizing the need to create different types of learning within group counselling, the group is more likely to meet the primary learning needs of individuals with different learning styles.

1. *Reflecting on Experience* calls upon learners to recall their own experience related to current learning. This activates the knowledge a learner already possesses and increases attention and motivation for new learning. This learning process builds a bridge from the past to the current learning environment. Reflecting on experience is expected to result in recognition of universality and instillation of hope.

   a. *Sharing by Members* - Members are encouraged to share about either recent events or past struggles that continue to impact them. Example: Start the group with a check-in and have members report about their weeks, paying particular attention to following up on any plans for action that were made the past week.

   b. *Identification of Theme* - It is often helpful for the group facilitator to identify the theme that one or more group members are exploring. This encourages the recognition of similarity or universality. Example: Common themes that come up in groups that can be highlighted by a facilitator include social isolation, self-doubts, unrecognized or unexpressed feelings, self-defeating thoughts or behaviours, or unfulfilled hopes or dreams.

c. *Recognition of Similarity* - As one group member shares, others are encouraged to reflect on times when they have had similar experiences, thoughts or feelings. Technique: "Reflect Around" As one member shares about feeling socially isolated, the facilitator asks other group members to think about and verbally identify times when they have each felt isolated. Technique: "Group Survey" The facilitator asks group members to raise their hand to indicate whether they have shared a common experience. For example, after one group member shares about fear of failure, group members are asked how many others have secretly feared that they would not succeed.

2. *Assimilating and Conceptualizing* provides learners with new information, theories or concepts and encourages learners to apply this knowledge to their own life experience. There is a reciprocal process in which the new concepts enhance a learner's self understanding and the process of comparing the concepts to oneself helps a learner understand the concepts more deeply. This learning process builds a bridge between theoretical concepts and individual experience. Assimilating and conceptualizing is similar to Yalom's therapeutic factor of imparting information.

a. *Learning from other Group Members* - An individual can ask for input from other group members that may include advice, suggestions or resources. Example: When discussing separation from parents, a group member asks for suggestions about setting appropriate limits.

b. *Conceptual Template* - A facilitator may suggest the use of concepts, categories or language that may help clarify group content. Example: If one or more group members are expressing a desire not to let themselves be pushed around, it may be helpful for the facilitator to talk about and define the concepts of passive, aggressive and assertive behaviour.

3. *Experimenting and Practicing* allows learners to try new behaviours and practice new skills within the context of a supportive learning environment. There is also the opportunity for suggestions and feedback from other learners. This learning process builds a bridge from abstract ideas to specific behaviours. Experimenting and practicing is related to several of Yalom's therapeutic factors including development of socializing techniques, imitative behaviour, catharsis and interpersonal learning.

a. *Experiments within Group* - A group member is encouraged to try new behaviour within the group that they may not usually display. Example: A group member who has a hard time giving compliments is encouraged to go around the group and tell each other member something that they like or appreciate.

b. *Role Playing* - In preparing for new behaviour outside the group, a group member uses other members to rehearse and to generate ideas to be used in the future. Example: A group member who is anxious about asking someone out on a date has a chance to practice what to say with another member playing the role of the potential date. Other group members can provide feedback or suggestions.

c. *Psychodramatic Experiments* - A group member may act out past conflicts or a symbolic representation of internal conflicts. Example: A group member confronts his dead mother and tells her that he can no longer actively grieve her and that he must move on with his life.

4. *Planning for Application* identifies areas of personal relevance and encourages learners to prepare for the transition from the group learning environment to real life. Specificity of planning increases the likelihood of transfer of learning. This learning process builds a bridge from the group to concrete experience in the future. Planning for application increases the likelihood that interpersonal learning will be generalized outside of the group.

   a. *Generalizing and Applying* - Group members identify areas where the things discussed in group can be generalized and applied. Example: After talking about ways of controlling anger, members identify areas where each method would be most helpful.

   b. *Planning for Action* - Group members make specific plans for changes they will make as a result of learning in group. Example: After talking about friendship development, each group member shares one thing they plan to do to reach out to a friend during the coming week.

The application of Kolb's model of experiential learning to group counselling is a useful guide to strategies that can occur within a single group counselling session. The following is a recent example of a group session in which the counsellors were able to promote all four experiential learning processes in one session:

Reflecting on Experience:

— *Identification of Theme*. During the second session of a men's counselling group, two members mentioned concerns related to anger at check-in. After one member had described a recent experience, anger was identified as a common theme by one of the facilitators. This theme was described in a way that optimised the universality of the emotion while recognizing that different situations or events will lead to anger for different members and that methods of expression would also differ.

— *Reflect Around*. After the theme was identified, one of the facilitators asked the group members to go around the circle and each identify things that most frequently make them angry. Commonalties within the theme were identified before focusing again on concerns of individual group members.

Assimilating and Conceptualizing

— *Conceptual Template*. After one member had talked about how anger sometimes is a response to fear, one of the facilitators described the pattern in which men frequently experience or express anger in place of more vulnerable emotions such as fear or sadness. After suggesting this conceptual template, the facilitator suggested another reflect around during which group members disclosed whether this pattern was true for them and described the types of vulnerable emotions that were frequently masked by anger.

Experimenting and Practicing

— *Role Playing*. One member of the group described a recent situation in which he felt afraid but responded with anger and swearing. This member was asked by one of the facilitators if he would like to participate in an experiment in which he would get a chance to replay the situation the way he would like to have behaved. The member was encouraged to choose two other group members as actors to play the roles of others in the situation. The member then acted out the scene in a new way allowing him to experiment with new ways of behaving and practice this behaviour in a supportive environment. When the member felt stuck, the facilitators encouraged him to ask for suggestions from the group. Feedback from group members was encouraged after the role play.

Planning for Application

— *Action Plan*. At the end of the group, members were encouraged to set personal goals regarding the way they would like to deal with anger and other emotions during the coming week. At check-in the following week, group members were given the opportunity to update the group on how well they accomplished their goals.

11 Group Facilitation Skills

Leadership is the process of assisting a group to realise its common goals, visions, and dreams. Effective leaders capitalise on the talents and diverse ideas of the group members to formulate and achieve these goals. Leadership involves encouraging a group to develop and grow by creating opportunities for group members to learn from one another through common experiences. In order to accomplish all of this, a leader needs to possess strong group facilitation skills. Group facilitation skills are the things that a leader says or does to promote experiential learning within a group. These skills will enable a leader to guide a group through the complex stages of group development, creating a cohesive team that learns from experience.

As a university student leader, you will be called on to use your facilitation skills in a variety of settings such as a resident advisor conducting a hall meeting, an orientation leader guiding a campus tour, a peer educator presenting a health education workshop, or an officer of a student organisation planning an event. Whatever your role as a student leader, strong facilitation skills will enable you to foster positive group interaction and individual learning.

The examples of facilitation skills described later will draw upon the experience of five types of student leaders:

— Peer Mentors who work in orientation, learning communities, or advising

— Peer Educators who present on health, academic, or personal growth topics

— Student Government Leaders who serve on representative bodies or advisory boards

— Club & Organisation Leaders who are involved in social, cultural / ethnic, political, religious, fraternity/ sorority, service, or sports / recreation groups for students

— Resident Advisors and other student leaders who work in residential programmes

The facilitation skills outlined here can be applied to a variety of settings in which university student leaders interact with groups. For example, student leaders frequently facilitate groups in the following four settings:

— Meetings—student government, hall meetings, student groups, staff meetings, etc.

— Presentations—academic skills, health education, advising, student government, etc.

— Discussion Groups—learning communities, residential life, student groups, etc.

— Work Teams—planning committees, task force groups, group assignments in classes, etc.

— Informal Groups—hanging out, eating lunch, campus tours, campus activities, etc.

Individual Learning Styles

David Kolb described a model of experiential learning that provides a useful way to think about leadership and group facilitation. Kolb described four ways that people learn which he referred to as concrete experience, reflective observation, abstract conceptualisation, and active experimentation. He arranged these four learning modes in a circle and suggested that effective learning involves completing this experiential learning cycle. We encourage you to think of promoting experiential learning as an essential aspect of your role as a student leader.

Kolb also used these learning modes as anchors on two perpendicular axes to identify four individual learning styles. McCarthy applied this model to education and referred to these leaning styles as imaginative, analytic, common sense and dynamic learners. As a student leader, it is important to realise that different group members will have different learning styles which will impact the way they behave in a group. To be an effective group leader, you should be aware of these four learning styles and learn to use skills that will meet the needs of all group members.

Imaginative Learners are oriented toward concrete experience and reflective observation. They have strengths in imaginative ability and awareness of meaning and values. Imaginative learners learn best when they are given the opportunity for personal involvement and interpersonal interaction.

Analytic Learners are oriented toward abstract conceptualisation and reflective observation. They have strengths in inductive reasoning and creating theoretical models. Analytic learners like to learn about theories, facts, concepts, and data and often excel in traditional educational settings.

Common Sense Learners are oriented toward abstract conceptualisation and active experimentation. They have strengths in problem solving and decision making. They want to put learning to immediate practical use. Common Sense learners want to be involved in hands-on learning that involves experimenting with new knowledge.

Dynamic Learners are oriented toward concrete experience and active experimentation. They have strengths related to carrying out plans, taking action, and getting involved with new experiences. Dynamic learners may be anxious to know how to apply new learning and will want to put ideas into action.

Facilitation Skills

Brooks-Harris and Stock-Ward used Kolb's model of experiential learning and individual learning styles to identify four types of facilitation skills. They are referred to here as engaging, informing, involving, and planning skills. Engaging skills correspond to imaginative learning, informing skills promote analytic learning, involving skills match common sense learning, and planning skills correspond to dynamic learning. We have adapted Brooks-Harris and Stock-Ward's model specifically to student leadership in order to identify 20 facilitation skills for you to learn, practice, and use in your groups. An effective group leader should develop all four types of facilitation skills.

Attending Skills

Attending skills are communication skills that form a foundation for group facilitation. Attending involves active listening skills that can help you make contact with another person and hear how they understand the world. These skills were originally identified to train individual counselors but they also are essential to group facilitation. As a student leader, it is important to develop strong attending skills to communicate with both individuals and groups. These skills are used to support all four types of group learning: engaging, informing, involving, and planning. Ivey, Gluckstern, and Ivey identified five types of basic attending skills:

— *Active Listening with Attending Behaviors*—Active listening involves verbal and nonverbal behaviors that demonstrate you are listening and encourages another person to talk more freely. Attending behaviors include appropriate eye contact, attentive body language, and using a vocal style that indicates interest.

— *Open Invitation to Talk*—By asking open questions, you can encourage someone to talk more freely. An open question is one that allows the other person to elaborate on information of their choice. In contrast, a closed question emphasises content and can often be answered in a few words or with a yes or no. Open questions are preferred because they allow you to follow the lead of the person to whom you are listening.

— *Encouraging and Paraphrasing*—You can clarify what someone is saying by using a verbal minimal encourage such as "Uh-huh," "Really?," or "Tell me more." You can also clarify by paraphrasing what someone says in order to let them know that they have been heard. For example, "Mandy, you're disappointed because we didn't get to finish the discussion, is that right?"

— *Reflecting Feelings*—It is often helpful to identify emotions that are expressed indirectly. This involves focusing more on the feeling than the content. For example, "It seems like you're really angry that this programme was canceled." Key emotions include happiness, sadness, anger, and fear.

— *Summarisation*—The purpose of summarisation is to help another individual integrate behavior, thoughts, and feelings. For example, "After you turned in the petition and it was rejected, you thought you were treated unfairly and you're afraid that you won't get another chance. Is that what you said?"

Group Facilitation Skills vs. Attending Skills

Group facilitation skills go one step further than attending skills. Attending skills are used to ensure a good connection between a listener and a speaker. Group facilitation skills are designed to create a sense of connection within an entire group and between group members as well as with the leader. You will use attending skills in all four types of group facilitation but you will be taking an extra step to focus on the whole group and not just the individuals within the group.

Types of Group Facilitation Skills

Being an effective group leader involves using skills that allow you to influence the way a group interacts and learns. These skills are collectively referred to as "Group Facilitation Skills." In order to develop these skills, you will need to identify, learn, and practice a wide variety of specific behaviors that promote positive group interactions. This section will describe four types of facilitation skills that promote different types of experiential learning. The model represented here assumes that an effective group leader has facilitation skills appropriate for promoting different types of interactive learning.

Engaging Facilitation Skills invite members to be a part of a group. They encourage a member to feel included and valued within the group context. These skills help individuals make the transition from their past experiences into a new context. They help group members reflect on what they already know and prepare them for interactive learning. Engaging skills are used to create curiosity, interest and energy. They encourage the discovery of personal meaning and interpersonal connections.

Informing Facilitation Skills are used to provide a group with information from outside the group and to help the group learn about itself. These skills include teaching factual information and allowing group members to gain new knowledge. Two types of information are relevant to a group learning format; first, content information from outside the group and, second, process information from within the group itself.

Involving Facilitation Skills encourage positive interaction and learning between group members. These skills create an opportunity for active experimentation and encourage learning by practice and allow group members to put new knowledge to practical use. Because involvement occurs when group members themselves practice and gain hands-on experience, these facilitation skills require a shift in focus away from the leader and toward the group and the members within the group.

Planning Facilitation Skills focus on planning for the future and applying learning from the group to other contexts. These skills encourage members to work together to make specific plans to accomplish group or individual goals. Planning skills prepare group members to move from active experimentation within the group to concrete experience beyond the group.

Group Facilitation Skills for Student Leaders

Engaging facilitation skills

— *Demonstrating Leadership*—letting the group know who's in charge

— *Creating an Open Environment*—inviting people to be a part of the group

— *Encouraging Connections*—helping people get acquainted and connected

— *Building Group Rapport*—facilitating a sense of teamwork and unity

— *Defining Group Identity*—establishing the group purpose and personality

Informing facilitation skills

— Providing Information—presenting facts, resources, knowledge, theories, or data

— Soliciting Information—asking questions, surveying ideas, or gathering data

— Clarifying Ideas or Concepts—making sure everyone is on the same wavelength

— Conceptualising—using new knowledge to better understand the group

— Learning from Within the Group—gathering information about the group itself

Involving facilitation skills

— Inviting Participation and Interaction—prompting action, contact, and dialogue

— Bouncing Back to the Group—shifting focus away from the leader

— Recognising Commonalities & Promoting Consensus—finding common ground

— Supporting Cooperation & Group Cohesion—fostering group unity

— Experimenting with New Behavior—encouraging members to try new things

Planning facilitation skills

— *Brainstorming*—identifying multiple possibilities

— *Generalising*—taking experience from one area and trying it in another

— *Strategising*—determining the best way to approach an issue

— *Applying*—putting knowledge into action or taking learning with you

— *Making Specific Plans*—creating an action plan

Examples of Engaging Facilitation Skills

Demonstrating Leadership : This skill identifies you as the leader and let's group members know that you'll provide guidance, support, and structure for the group. Example: "Hey everybody, I'd like your attention! I'm Jordan and I'm going to be your orientation leader for the next two days."

Creating an Open Environment : There are things you can do as a leader to welcome new members to the group and make them feel included. Example: "I'm really glad that each of you are going to be living on the 9th floor of Aloha Tower this year. I think we're going to have a great time together. I'd like to go around the group and have everyone share one thing they're looking forward to at UH this year."

Encouraging Connections : In order to feel connected to a group, members need to get to know one another and see what they have in common. Example: "I'd like each of the representatives here to introduce themselves and say a few things about the group they represent and what other groups here they interact with the most."

Building Group Rapport : One of the challenges of group leadership is creating camaraderie and good will within the group. It is important to encourage positive interactions that make members feel good about being part of the group. Example: "Thanks for coming to this time management workshop. Since I'm sure we all procrastinate, I'd like each of us to share one thing that we do to waste time when we're avoiding something more important."

Defining Group Identity : Every group has an identity and an atmosphere. As a leader, you will set the tone for defining what the group is all about and what it will feel like to be a member. Example: "Let me tell you about what the kayak club has been like and what we've done in the past and then we can talk about whether we want to do the same things this year."

Examples of Informing Facilitation Skills

Providing Information : Leadership often involves providing the group with pertinent information that they don't already have. This information might include facts, resources, knowledge, theories, or data. A lecture is one of many ways to provide information. Example: "There are several resources on campus that can help support our group activities. Let me tell you about some of them..."

Soliciting Information: A leader often needs to collect information from the group members. This can be done by asking open ended questions, surveying ideas, or gathering data. Example: "What kinds of things have you done to effectively manage your stress in the past? Can I have two or three people share what has worked for them?"

Clarifying Ideas or Concepts: This skill involves making sure everyone understands what is being said or agreed upon. One way to clarify is to summarise the concept or idea and see if there are any misunderstandings. Example: "Let me make sure that I am clear on this. We would like to have quiet hours from 6:30 p.m. to 9:30 p.m. and then from 10:00 p.m. to 8:00 a.m. Is that what we're all agreeing on?"

Conceptualising : Being a leader sometimes involves using new or outside knowledge to help the group better understand itself. Looking at the group using a particular theory, model, or concept is one example of conceptualising. Example: "In my leadership class, I just learned about three styles of leadership. In our group, I think there is a conflict between those who favor an authoritarian style and those who prefer laissez-faire leadership."

Learning from Within the Group: In addition to providing information from outside the group, you can survey group members or gather information about the group itself. You might also use your observation skills to identify group characteristics, themes, or process. Example: "In addition to the examples of study skills from the book, I'd like for us to identify our own skills. Let's go around the group and have each person identify one good study habit and one bad study habit they need to change."

Examples of Involving Facilitation Skills

Inviting Participation and Interaction : Leadership often involves prompting group members to take action or to interact with one another. This interaction can occur within the present group or in the future. Example: "Let's break down into small groups so that everyone can share their ideas about how to better promote spiritual growth on campus."

Bouncing Back to the Group : The group's attention may naturally gravitate toward you as the leader. However, it is often helpful for you to deflect this attention and "bounce" the focus or energy back to the group itself to keep interaction and involvement high. Example: "That's a really good question. What have other people's experiences been in this situation?"

Recognising Commonalities and Promoting Consensus : Promoting involvement often involves helping group members find similarities in ideas, interests, values, and plans. Conflicts often arise when the group focuses on differences rather than common ground. Identifying similarities can be used to support common goals. Example: "It sounds like you have different ideas about how clean you need your room to be but you both agree that you want to work this out and maintain a friendship. After hearing from both of you, let's agree on some minimum standards that would be mutually agreeable."

Supporting Cooperation and Group Cohesion : As the identity of the group continues to form and strengthen, a key leadership skill is to encourage supportive interactions and nurture the ongoing interdependence of the members so that they feel like they can accomplish more as a group than individually. Example: "As we continue to lobby against tuition raises, it is important that we show a united front. We need to make sure that we are supporting each other and communicating the same message. How should we present our collective point of view?"

Experimenting with New Behavior : Group learning often involves encouraging members to try new things. Experimenting can include role plays, work sheets, or other exercises as well as simply suggesting alternate behaviors for members to try. Example: "Now that we've talked about different ways to meet people on campus, I'd like to do some role plays. Who would like to practice some of these skills?"

Examples of Planning Facilitation Skills

Brainstorming : One of the best ways for a group to start the planning process is by generating lots of ideas in a nonevaluative manner. Brainstorming allows a group to think of a diverse and large number of ideas in a short period of time without rejecting ideas too quickly. Example: "We need to think of some possible fund-raisers for the Spring semester. Let's shout out as many different ideas as possible without criticising the ideas. We can go back and evaluate how realistic each idea is later."

Generalising : This skill involves taking a successful behavior from one area and trying it in a new area. Example: "Now that we've all identified strategies that we used to achieve important goals in the past, let's see which of these strategies will help you achieve academic success here at UH."

Strategising : After analysing a problem and brainstorming possible solutions, it is important to make a decision about the best way to solve a problem or approach a challenge. Example: "It seems like there is too much underage drinking in our halls because there aren't any fun alternatives to alcohol on the weekend. Let's think about other things students like to do and see what we can plan."

Applying : Once knowledge has been shared in a group, it should be put into action in a way that directly relates to the experience of the group. In this way, group members can take new learning home with them. Example: "Now that we've talked about the importance of verbally communicating about sex in order to prevent negative consequences like STDs and coercion, I'd like each of you to write down some things a student could actually say to a dating partner to bring up these topics... Does anyone want to share what they've written?"

Making Specific Plans : Creating an action plan with specific steps, a time-line, and designation of who is going to take the lead on each section is a crucial skill in helping a group realise its goals. Example: "Now that we have passed legislation to spend money on improving library services, what specific steps are we going to take to accomplish this goal? Let's write them on the board and then assign leaders and a time-line."

Leadership Techniques that Support Group Facilitation

— *Checking-In/Round Robin*—To ensure complete participation, it may be helpful to go around the group and have each member take a turn sharing.

— *Writing*—Writing can be used as a way for members to privately organise their thoughts before sharing with the larger group. One way to do this is by handing out index cards and having members record their thoughts.

— *Using Humor*—To build group rapport, you may want to use some moderate and appropriate humor. Humor should be used to create safety and not alienate or offend people in the group.

— *Self-Disclosing*—At times, it is appropriate to share your own experience as an example or model. Self disclosure can also be used to build rapport with the group by highlighting your similarity to group members.

— *Surveying / Voting*—One way to gather information about a group is to survey all the members or to have them vote on a particular issue or idea.

— *Modeling*—Demonstrating skills and/or behavior is an active way of providing information to a group that prepares them for practice or other forms of involvement.

— *Sharing in Pairs / Small Groups*—Breaking the group into pairs or small groups allows all members to share their ideas in a less-threatening environment. After sharing in a small group, some members may find it more comfortable to share their ideas with the large group. Common themes can then be identified in an open discussion.

— *Critiquing / Giving Feedback*—One way to involve group members is to ask them to give feedback or to critique what you or others have said or done. It is important to encourage the group to start with strengths or positive feedback before suggesting areas for improvement.

— *Role Playing*—A great way to encourage new behavior is to ask group members to actually act out what they would do or say in a particular situation. Other group members can play other roles to flesh out the situation.

Strategies for Improving Your Facilitation Skills

— *Identify Your Own Learning Style*—Complete Kolb's Learning Style Inventory to assess your learning preferences. Your leadership style may emphasise your preferences and overlook the needs of other styles.

— *Consider the Diversity of Learning Styles in Your Group*—Remember that people in your group probably have a range of learning styles. This will help you adapt various approaches to facilitation that meet diverse learning needs.

— *Reflect on Your Strengths and Weaknesses*—Review the list of 20 facilitation skills and make note of those that you consider personal strengths and those that need the most improvement.

— *Target Specific Skills for Practice*—Look over the skills you have identified for improvement or addition and decide which skills you should work on first. It is best to target no more than two or three at a time.

— *Practice Skills in a Safe Environment*—Identify a safe place, such as a leadership class, where it is okay to make mistakes and experiment with new techniques. This is the ideal way to start practicing new skills.

— *Identify Opportunities in Your Group to Improve or Try New Skills*—Seek out diverse opportunities to practice facilitation in your group. Volunteer to facilitate a portion of your next meeting or give a presentation. Look for opportunities to practice facilitation skills in informal interactions with group members as well.

— *Ask Someone to Observe and Give You Feedback*—Ask another leader to observe your facilitation skills and give you constructive feedback on what you did well and what you can improve.

— *Observe Other Leaders*—Watch other leaders facilitate a group to discover ways to enhance your own skills. Use the Group Facilitation Skills Checklist to keep track of the skills you observe.

— *Videotape Yourself and Evaluate Your Skill Usage*—Observe yourself on videotape to assess and improve your leadership.

12

Group Counselling for Mental Retardation

Although many clinicians have not regarded people with mental retardation as suitable candidates for any form of psychotherapy there are many case reports on the effectiveness of individual psychotherapy as well as for group psychotherapy. Psychotherapy for people with mental retardation has been most effective when a directive style with structured sessions is used. Additionally the use of active/interactive techniques stimulates more sensory and affective modes of learning than the verbal modality alone.

Despite the evidence of effectiveness and recommendations by researchers to use a group method, group psychotherapy for people with mental retardation is usually not considered as a viable therapeutic modality. Historically, the research on this matter showed that people with mental retardation could not profit from insight oriented interactive therapy because they lacked specific cognitive abilities thought necessary for therapeutic change. While this may be the primary reason that psychotherapy is overlooked as a treatment modality for people with mental retardation, there have been a series of erroneous assumptions on the part of practitioners. Consider the following major suppositions:

1. Since many developmentally disabled people are not verbal (or have difficulty verbalising) they are thought to be unable to produce clues to regulating their behaviour.
2. The secondary disabilities that often are associated with mental retardation (short attention span, auditory and visual handicaps, seizure activity, etc.) are thought to provide insurmountable obstacles to interactive group therapy.
3. People with mental retardation lack the cognitive ability to profit from insight into the causes and consequences of their behaviour.
4. Many practitioners understand the emotional disorders displayed by people with mental retardation as a side effect of a biochemical brain dysfunction. As such they feel there is little that psychotherapy can offer.
5. Somehow the emotional and behavioral problems of people with mental retardation are understood as being the result of mental illness or behaviour disorder. With such elementary discriminations only psychopharmacological or behavioral treatments alone are sought. The use of psychotherapy to help ameliorate these problems is rarely considered.

The reality is that even if an astute and aware clinician were to recommend psychotherapy the task of finding someone knowledgeable and competent to deliver such services would often be a difficult job. Although more and more providers are beginning groups and developing their group skills, group psychotherapy is only now beginning to emerge as a treatment option on a wider scale. One other reason why group therapy is the least used therapy for people with mental retardation (in addition to the ones listed above) may be that the dissemination of information on how to do such counselling was limited by the scarcity of research showing which method(s) were effective. In other words while there may have been good indications that group therapy could be possible, volume of such information was not sufficient to offset the assumptions of practitioners.

Advantages of Group Therapy

The time has come for greater attention to be given to the group process. To begin with, using group counselling for people with mental retardation makes good clinical and economic sense. Consider the advantages of using a group format:

1. The skills to run an effective group can be taught in a brief period of time (2-3 months for a novice and considerably less for the more experienced).
2. In the same amount of time it takes to run a teaching based skill-training group a more richly interactive group can take place through facilitation rather than teaching.
3. More people can be served in a group counselling format than can be served in an individual setting.
4. It can be argued that the treatment in a group is more effective than individual counselling.
5. On all pay scales, the cost to an individual for group psychotherapy is cheaper than individual therapy.
6. Specific topics may target selected groups for particular problems (anger management groups, sex offender

groups, bereavement groups, job readiness, etc.) In this way people with similar issues may gain support in ways not possible in individual counselling.

7. This kind of peer support is not limited to homogeneous groups. Interpersonal support from peers struggling with different issues is not available in any other format.

Interactive-Behavioural Model

The Interactive-Behavioral Model has focused on fourteen therapeutic factors that have empirical validity with respect to group therapy in general. A therapeutic factor is defined as a component of group therapy that benefits a member's condition. This improvement comes as a result of actions by the group facilitator, the members, and the individual him or herself. These factors are follows:

1. Acceptance/cohesion
2. Universality
3. Altruism
4. Installation of hope
5. Guidance
6. Vicarious Learning/Modelling
7. Catharsis
8. Imparting of information
9. Self-Disclosure
10. Self-understanding
11. Interpersonal learning
12. Corrective Recapitulation of the Primary Family

13. Development of Socialising Techniques
14. Existential Factors

The Interactive-Behavioral Model uses these therapeutic factors, which are the most effective and well established features of group psychotherapy, and establishes their presence and vitalisation within groups for people with mental retardation. What has evolved is a four stage format for group psychotherapy which adapts processes and techniques that are effective with other populations, while introducing interventions created specifically for people with mental retardation.

This model uses a 45-minute to one-hour, four stage arrangement. It combines theoretically sound techniques for activating therapeutic factors from the field of psychodrama with some modifications specific to people with dual diagnosis (e.g., the orientation and affirmation stages). The four stages of this model are:

1) orientation;
2) warm-up and sharing;
3) enactment; and
4) affirmation.

The Orientation Stage

The orientation stage was designed to help with the initial difficulty encountered in establishing a group with the potential for therapeutic factors to emerge. Poor eye contact, difficulty with short-term recognition or memory, impaired hearing, delayed responding, confusion, echolalia, inattention, distractibility, speech impediments and hyperactivity are just some of the obstacles to interaction between members.

It, therefore, becomes a primary function of the facilitators to do what is called "cognitive networking." This is an effort to establish basic interactions between and among the group's members by having them repeat, acknowledge or otherwise support what was said by another member in the group. Physically orienting towards the person speaking, looking at them and echoing back what was heard are central elements to cognitive networking.

This process begins in the orientation stage but will continue throughout the group. Without such rudimentary interaction there is a diminished opportunity for therapeutic factors to emerge and be reinforced. As such, the orientation stage is characterised by the facilitator(s) assisting members in interacting with each other and participating in the group process. Having members repeat what was said to them, turn toward the person speaking, acknowledge what was said, and/or in some way participate in the group process through interaction is the goal of this first stage. If the members fail to attend to each other, any other therapeutic, corrective, or instructional goals within the group will not be realised.

The Warm-Up and Sharing Stage

The second stage of the group ushers in more intimate interactions between members. In the warm-up and sharing stage the facilitator invites the members to speak within the group. This is a process-driven group, and as such, the content of their presentations is of less importance. In other words, the facilitator's concern is with the dynamics of the group. The facilitator's job is to pay attention to the nature of the interactions between the various members. During this second stage the group members take turns making their self-disclosures, and the cognitive networking begun in the orientation stage is continued. For example, the facilitator may ask the member, who has just finished speaking, to select the next member to go. In this way, members are again encouraged to pay attention to and interact with each other rather than with the facilitator exclusively.

Following this level of participation, the facilitator will then ask the members if any of them has a problem to work on in the group. It is during this deeper level of sharing that the members will experience a greater sense of emotional involvement within the group. The group becomes more cohesive, and the stage is set for action to take place.

The Enactment Stage

The central feature of the Interactive-Behavioral Model is the enactment stage. All of the features of the enactment stage are modifications derived from the field of psychodrama. Psychodrama is a particular type of group psychotherapy. It involves both theory and techniques. In fact, psychodrama is the original form of group work developed by the creator of the term "group therapy," Jacob Moreno, M.D.

Over the years techniques from psychodrama (reflecting issues unique to an individual's life) and sociodrama (issues which reflect a collective concern) have been used with people with mental retardation. However, the primary use of role playing was for role training. More specifically, these techniques were used almost exclusively for social-skills training rather than for the purpose of facilitating therapeutic interactions. The teachers in these groups fostered interaction between themselves and the participants rather than between and among the participants. Since the emphasis was on teaching a skill, the attention had to be focused on the teacher/trainer. In the interactive-behavioral format, the emphasis is on interaction between the participants for the purpose of creating a therapeutic environment. As such there is a major shift from a teaching/training model to a peer support/interaction model where behaviours having therapeutic value are reinforced as a way of strengthening viable group processes.

It is during the enactment stage that techniques such as role playing and the double are used. The issues presented in the warm-up and sharing stage are formulated into characters with the help of the facilitator. Although only certain group members may take part in the enactment, the entire group's focus of attention is on the action taking place. Of the four stages, the enactment stage is the core focus of the group. Within the enactment stage there are a number of techniques used to stimulate interaction between group members.

One of the most useful of those techniques is the double. Broadly stated, a double is a role played by one or more group members as they give voice to the feelings and thoughts of another member who is struggling with a given problem. The use of the double can be a tremendous asset in groups for people with mental retardation, chronic psychiatric illness and dual diagnoses. The double has several purposes. It can provide emotional support, give emotional expression and/or reorganise perceptions. The process and techniques used in doubling include speaking the unspoken (what the person needs to say but is not saying), exaggerating, minimising, introducing alternatives, restating, amplifying (highlighting the key part of the statement), verbalising the resistance (why the person doesn't want to say something) and introducing paradoxes.

The Affirmation Stage

Finally, in the affirmation stage the facilitator validates the participation of each of the members in the group. This is done with specific attention to the therapeutic factors. Each member is verbally acknowledged for his or her interactive contributions to the group. This reinforces the member's new social skills and has the added benefit of helping the affective intensity of the enactment stage to scale down somewhat.

Obstacles of Using Group Counselling

With all these potential advantages it would appear that group therapy should be given a more central role in treatment planning. While this is slowly beginning to happen, there are still a few obstacles which may be inhibiting the use of group counselling. The first and perhaps greatest of these obstacles may be empirical. In general the entire field of group psychotherapy struggles with scientific validation of process and outcome. Even sophisticated publications on the mechanics of running and maintaining a group leave out any mention of the validity of the group process. The challenge before those who are involved in group work with people with mental retardation is to provide data showing the similarities and differences between these groups and those with non-developmentally disabled people. Additionally, the necessary modifications as well as the effectiveness of the process on behaviour outside of group must be addressed.

The evaluation of the effectiveness of group therapy is arguably the most difficult of all therapeutic validation efforts. Process and outcome research is greatly hampered by issues surrounding criteria, meaningful dependent variables and proper methodology. Indeed the difficulty in assessment of psychotherapy has been related by Nuffield to be attributed to the following conditions: "[t]he fuzzy and poor description of the therapeutic process, the inadequate description of the context, the failure to describe the intercurrent events that may be important, and the lack of objective outcome measures that are meaningful and that can be considered to be empirically valid."

In using group therapy for people with mental retardation the question of validity becomes more critical to demonstrate, yet more difficult to design. This difficulty has not been encountered directly perhaps due to the fundamental difference between training and counselling. As prior indications were that group work was not an appropriate means of therapy, the need for skill development was installed as the chief function of the group meeting. Role playing was most often used as the primary vehicle for instruction. The criteria became clear as to the effectiveness of the group. Could the person demonstrate the skill rehearsed in the training group? If so, the group was successful. If not, another facilitator, another group, or another strategy were employed.

The current state of development reflects a need for a shift from "training" group approach to a more interactive and therapeutic counselling format. In doing this the emphasis on evaluating the acquisition of a particular skill with an individual in the group remains an important criteria for determining the effectiveness of the group process. However, the exclusive focusing on specific skill development often neglects the rich potential to provide generalised support, (not limited to specific skill acquisition) on-going encouragement, a sense of belongingness, hope and other (re)habilitative elements that accompany a positive group experience.

The transformation is from content driven skill oriented groups, to those which are focused on process. This shift would seem to require that a type of concurrent validity be established. By this we mean to take what has been accomplished in group therapy in general and extrapolate from these findings for groups with people with mental retardation. This approach has been identified as a primary vehicle for making group psychotherapy available to mentally retarded persons by Pfadt. Along these lines and particularly with regard to process, Yalom along with Bloch and Crouch have advanced one of the most comprehensive research based investigations of group psychotherapy available.

Yalom has proposed that a collection of therapeutic factors account for the effectiveness of a group. These factors, when present, indicate the viability of group process, and consequently, the therapeutic potential for group members. A logical place to begin then would be to look for these factors in groups for people with dual diagnosis and further, to look for those efforts which activate these factors. Since process would then be viewed (at least initially) as more essential than content, two important questions concerning the validity of the process emerge.

The shift towards group counselling from skill training groups may require that the content of the group become secondary to its process. The Interactive-Behavioral Model has enjoyed wide usage. To a great degree this is due to the fact the model describes a process taken from well established principles in group psychotherapy that have been modified for people with mental retardation. It, therefore, can be adapted for use with various curricula. Examples include: anger management; AIDS awareness training; relationship counselling; sexual abuse avoidance training; mental health counselling; vocational readiness; behaviour management; travel training; independent living readiness; sex education; socialisation; educational readiness; parent-child education; birth control; and advocacy groups. Such a broad base use of the model seems to indicate that the four stage process of the group is more essential to the functioning of the group than is the content of the group. The presence of therapeutic factors within the groups sets the stage for corrective work to be done. Future research should focus on the validity of the process of the groups run for people with mental retardation.

13

Gestalt Therapy

Gestalt therapy is a phenomenological-existential therapy founded by Frederick (Fritz) and Laura Perls in the 1940s. It teaches therapists and patients the phenomenological method of awareness, in which perceiving, feeling, and acting are distinguished from interpreting and reshuffling preexisting attitudes. Explanations and interpretations are considered less reliable than what is directly perceived and felt. Patients and therapists in Gestalt therapy dialogue, that is, communicate their phenomenological perspectives. Differences in perspectives become the focus of experimentation and continued dialogue. The goal is for clients to become aware of what they are doing, how they are doing it, and how they can change themselves, and at the same time, to learn to accept and value themselves.

Phenomenological Perspectives of Gestalt Theory

Phenomenology is a discipline that helps people stand aside from their usual way of thinking so that they can tell the difference between what is actually being perceived and felt in the current situation and what is residue from the past. A Gestalt exploration respects, uses and clarifies immediate, "naive" perception "undebauched by learning". Gestalt therapy treats what is "subjectively" felt in the present, as well as what is "objectively" observed, as real and important data. This contrasts with approaches that treat what the patient experiences as "mere appearances" and uses interpretation to find "real meaning."

The goal of Gestalt phenomenological exploration is awareness, or insight. "Insight is a patterning of the perceptual field in such a way that the significant realities are apparent; it is the formation of a gestalt in which the relevant factors fall into place with respect to the whole". In Gestalt therapy insight is clear understanding of the structure of the situation being studied. Awareness without systematic exploration is not ordinarily sufficient to develop insight.

Therefore, Gestalt therapy uses focused awareness and experimentation to achieve insight. How one becomes aware is crucial to any phenomenological investigation. The phenomenologist studies not only personal awareness but also the awareness process itself. The patient is to learn how to become aware of awareness. How the therapist and the patient experience their relationship is of special concern in Gestalt therapy.

Perspective of Field Theory

The scientific world view that underlies the Gestalt phenomenological perspective is field theory. Field theory is a method of exploring that describes the whole field of which the event is currently a part rather than analysing the event in terms of a class to which it belongs by its "nature" (e.g., Aristotelian classification) or a unilinear, historical, cause-effect sequence (e.g., Newtonian mechanics). The field is a whole in which the parts are in immediate relationship and responsive to each other and no part is uninfluenced by what goes on elsewhere in the field. The field replaces the notion of discrete, isolated particles. The person in his or her life space constitutes a field.

In field theory no action is at a distance; that is, what has effect must touch that which is affected in time and space. Gestalt therapists work in the here and now and are sensitive to how the here and now includes residues of the past, such as body posture, habits, and beliefs. The phenomenological field is defined by the observer and is meaningful only when one knows the frame of reference of the observer. The observer is necessary because what one sees is somewhat a function of how and when one looks.

Field approaches are descriptive rather than speculative, interpretive, or classificatory. The emphasis is on observing, describing, and explicating the exact structure of whatever is being studied. In Gestalt therapy, data unavailable to direct observation by the therapist are studied by phenomenological focusing, experimenting, reporting of participants, and dialogue.

Perspectives of Existentialism

Existentialism is based on the phenomenological method. Existential phenomenologists focus on people's existence, relations with each other, joys and suffering, etc., as directly experienced. Most people operate in an unstated context of conventional thought that obscures or avoids acknowledging how the world is. This is especially true of one's relations in the world and one's choices. Self-deception is the basis of inauthenticity: living that is not based on the truth of oneself in the world leads to feelings of dread, guilt and anxiety.

Gestalt therapy provides a way of being authentic and meaningfully responsible for oneself. By becoming aware, one becomes able to choose and/or organise one's own existence in a meaningful manner. The existential view holds that people are endlessly remaking or discovering themselves. There is no essence of human nature to be discovered "once and for all." There are always new horizons, new problems and new opportunities.

Existential Dialogue

The relationship between the therapist and the client is the most important aspect of psychotherapy. Existential dialogue is an essential part of Gestalt therapy's methodology and is a manifestation of the existential perspective on relationship. Relationship grows out of contact. Through contact people grow and form identities. Contact is the experience of boundary between "me" and "not-me." It is the experience of interacting with the not-me while maintaining a self-identity separate from the not-me. Martin Buber states that the person ("I") has meaning only in relation to others, in the I-Thou dialogue or in I-It manipulative contact. Gestalt therapists prefer experiencing the patient in dialogue to using therapeutic manipulation (I-It).

Gestalt therapy helps clients develop their own support for desired contact or withdrawal. Support refers to anything that makes contact or withdrawal possible: energy, body support, breathing, information, concern for others, language, and so forth. Support mobilises resources for contact or withdrawal. For example, to support the excitement accompanying contact, a person must take in enough oxygen. The Gestalt therapist works by engaging in dialogue rather than by manipulating the patient toward some therapeutic goal. Such contact is marked by straightforward caring, warmth, acceptance and self-responsibility.

When therapists move patients toward some goal, the patients cannot be in charge of their own growth and self-support. Dialogue is based on experiencing the other person as he or she really is and showing the true self, sharing phenomenological awareness. The Gestalt therapist says what he or she means and encourages the patient to do the same. Gestalt dialogue embodies authenticity and responsibility.

The therapeutic relationship in Gestalt therapy emphasises four characteristics of dialogue:

1. *Inclusion*. This is putting oneself as fully as possible into the experience of the other without judging, analysing or interpreting while simultaneously retaining a sense of one's separate, autonomous presence. This is an existential and interpersonal application of the phenomenological trust in immediate experience. Inclusion provides an environment of safety for the patient's phenomenological work and, by communicating an understanding of the patient's experience, helps sharpen the patient's self-awareness.
2. *Presence*. The Gestalt therapist expresses herself to the patient. Regularly, judiciously, and with discrimination she expresses observations, preferences, feelings, personal experience and thoughts. Thus, the therapist shares her perspective by modelling phenomenological reporting, which aids the patient's learning about trust and use of immediate experience to raise awareness. If the therapist relies on theory-derived interpretation, rather than personal presence, she leads the patient into relying on phenomena not in his own immediate

experience as the tool for raising awareness. In Gestalt therapy the therapist does not use presence to manipulate the patient to conform to preestablished goals, but rather encourages patients to regulate themselves autonomously.

3. *Commitment to dialogue*. Contact is more than something two people do to each other. Contact is something that happens between people, something that arises from the interaction between them. The Gestalt therapist surrenders herself to this interpersonal process. This is allowing contact to happen rather than manipulating, making contact, and controlling the outcome.

4. *Dialogue is lived*. Dialogue is something done rather than talked about. "Lived" emphasises the excitement and immediacy of doing. The mode of dialogue can be dancing, song, words, or any modality that expresses and moves the energy between or among the participants. An important contribution of Gestalt therapy to phenomenological experimentation is enlarging the parameters to include explication of experience by nonverbal expressions. However, the interaction is limited by ethics, appropriateness, therapeutic task, and so on.

There are at least 62 Gestalt therapy institutes throughout the world, and the list continues to grow. Virtually every major city in the United States has at least one Gestalt institute. No national organisation has been established. As a result, there are no established standards for institutes, trainers and trainees. Each institute has its own criteria for training, membership selection, and so on. Attempts in the recent past to organise a nationwide conference for establishing standards for trainers have not been successful.

There are no agreed-upon standards for what constitutes good Gestalt therapy or a good Gestalt therapist. Therefore, it is incumbent on Gestalt therapy consumers to carefully evaluate the educational, clinical, and training background of people who call themselves Gestalt therapists or give training in Gestalt therapy. As experience in doing Gestalt therapy has grown, earlier therapeutic practices have been altered. For example, earlier Gestalt therapy practice often stressed the clinical use of frustration, a confusion of self-sufficiency with self-support, and an abrasive attitude if the patient was interpreted by the therapist as manipulative.

This approach tended to enhance the shame of shame-oriented patients. There has been a movement toward more softness in Gestalt therapy practice, more direct self-expression by the therapist, more of a dialogic emphasis, decreased use of stereotypic techniques, increased emphasis on description of character structure (with utilisation of psychoanalytic formulations), and increased use of group process.

Thus a patient is more likely to encounter, among Gestalt therapists who are involved in the newer mode, an emphasis on self-acceptance, a softer demeanour by the therapist, more trust of the patient's phenomenology, and more explicit work with psychodynamic themes. There has also been an increase in emphasis on group process, including relation between group members, and a decrease in formal, one-to-one work in groups. There is also an increased attention to theoretical instruction, theoretical exposition, and work with cognition in general.

THEORY OF PERSONALITY

A person exists by differentiating self from other and by

connecting self and other. These are the two functions of a boundary. To make good contact with one's world, it is necessary to risk reaching out and discovering one's own boundaries. Effective self-regulation includes contact in which one is aware of novelty in the environment that is potentially nourishing or toxic. That which is nourishing is assimilated and all else is rejected. This kind of differentiated contact inevitably leads to growth.

Mental Metabolism

In Gestalt therapy, metabolism is used as a metaphor for psychological functioning. People grow through biting off an appropriate-sized piece (be this food or ideas or relationships), chewing it (considering), and discovering whether it is nourishing or toxic. If nourishing, the organism assimilates it and makes it part of itself. If toxic, the organism spits it out (rejects it). This requires people to be willing to trust their taste and judgment. Discrimination requires actively sensing outside stimuli and processing these exteroceptive stimuli along with interoceptive data.

Regulation of the Boundary

The boundary between self and environment must be kept permeable to allow exchanges, yet firm enough for autonomy. The environment includes toxins to be screened out. Even what is nourishing needs to be discriminated according to the dominant needs. Metabolic processes are governed by the laws of homeostasis. Ideally, the most urgent need energises the organism untii it is met or is superseded by a more vital need. Living is a progression of needs, met and unmet, achieving homeostatic balance and going on to the next moment and new need.

Disturbances of the Contact Boundary

When the boundary between self and other becomes unclear, lost or impermeable, this results in a disturbance of the distinction between self and other, a disturbance of both contact and awareness. In good boundary functioning, people alternate between connecting and separating, between being in contact with the current environment and withdrawal of attention from the environment. The contact boundary is lost in polar opposite ways in confluence and isolation. In confluence (fusion), the separation and distinction between self and other becomes so unclear that the boundary is lost. In isolation, the boundary becomes so impermeable that connectedness is lost, i.e., the importance of others for the self is lost from awareness.

Retroflection is a split within the self, a resisting of aspects of the self by the self. This substitutes self for environment, as in doing to self what one wants to do to someone else or doing for self what one wants someone else to do for self. This mechanism leads to isolation. The illusion of self-sufficiency is one example of retroflection as it substitutes self for environment. Although one can do one's own breathing and chewing, the air and food must come from the environment. Introspection is a form of retroflection that can be pathological or healthy. For example, resisting the impulse to express anger may serve to cope with a dangerous environment. In such a situation, biting one's lip may be more functional than saying something biting.

Through introjection, foreign material is absorbed without discriminating or assimilating. Swallowing whole creates an "as if" personality and rigid character. Introjected values and behavior are imposed on self. As in all contact boundary disturbances, swallowing whole can be healthy or pathological, depending on the circumstances and degree of awareness. For example, students taking a lecture course may, with full awareness that they are doing so, copy, memorise and regurgitate material without full "digestion."

Projection is a confusion of self and other that results from attributing to the outside something that is truly self. An example of healthy projection is art. Pathological projection results from not being aware of and accepting responsibility for that which is projected.

Deflection is the avoidance of contact or of awareness by turning aside, as when one is polite instead of direct. Deflection can be accomplished by not expressing directly or by not receiving. In the latter case, the person usually feels "untouched"; in the former case, the person is often ineffective and baffled about not getting what is wanted. Deflection can be useful where, with awareness, it meets the needs of the situation (e.g., where the situation needs cooling down).

Organismic Self-Regulation

Human regulation is to varying degrees either (a) organismic, that is, based on a relatively full and accurate acknowledgment of what is, or (b) "shouldistic," based on the arbitrary imposition of what some controller thinks should or should not be. This applies to intrapsychic regulation, to the regulation of interpersonal relations and to the regulation of social groups.

"There is only one thing that should control: the situation, if you understand the situation you are in and let the situation you are in control our actions, then you learn to cope with life". Perls explicated the above with an example of driving a car. Instead of a preplanned program,

"I want to drive 65 miles per hour," a person cognizant of the situation will drive at different speed at night or differently when in traffic, or still differently when tired, and so on. Here Perls makes it clear that "let the situation control" means regulating through awareness of the contemporary context, including one's wants, rather than through what was thought "should" happen.

In organismic self-regulation, choosing and learning happen holistically, with a natural integration of mind and body, thought and feeling, spontaneity and deliberateness. In shouldistic regulation, cognition reigns and there is no felt, holistic sense. Obviously, everything relevant to boundary regulation cannot be in full awareness. Most transactions are handled by automatic, habitual modes, with minimal awareness. Organismic self-regulation requires that the habitual become fully aware as needed. When awareness does not emerge as needed and/or does not organise the necessary motor activity, psychotherapy is a method of increasing awareness and gaining meaningful choice and responsibility.

Awareness

Awareness and dialogue are the two primary therapeutic tools in Gestalt therapy. Awareness is a form of experience that may be loosely defined as being in touch with one's own existence, with what is. Full awareness is the process of being in vigilant contact with the most important events in the individual/environment field with full sensorimotor, emotional, cognitive and energetic support. Insight, a form of awareness, is an immediate grasp of the obvious unity of disparate elements in the field. Aware contact creates new, meaningful wholes and thus is in itself an integration of a problem.

Effective awareness is grounded in and energised by the dominant present need of the organism. It involves not only self-knowledge, but a direct knowing of the current situation and how the self is in that situation. Any denial of the situation and its demands or of one's wants and chosen response is a disturbance of awareness. Meaningful awareness is of a self in the world, in dialogue with the world, and with awareness of Other -- it is not an inwardly focused introspection. Awareness is accompanied by owning, that is, the process of knowing one's control over, choice of, and responsibility for one's own behavior and feelings.

Without this, the person may be vigilant to experience and life space, but not to what power he or she has and does not have. Awareness is cognitive, sensory and affective. The person who verbally acknowledges his situation but does not really see it, know it, react to it and feel in response to it is not fully aware and is not in full contact. The person who is aware knows what he does, how he does it, that he has alternatives and that he chooses to be as he is.

The act of awareness is always here and now, although the content of awareness may be distant. The act of remembering is now; what is remembered is not now. When the situation calls for an awareness of the past or anticipation of the future, effective awareness takes this into account.

Self-rejection and full awareness are mutually exclusive. Rejection of self is a distortion of awareness because it is a denial of who one is. Self-rejection is simultaneously a confusion of who "I am" and a self-deception, or "bad faith" attitude of being above that which is ostensibly being acknowledged. Saying "I am" as if it were an observation of another person, or as if the "I" were not chosen, or without knowing how one creates and perpetuates that "I am" is bad faith rather than insightful awareness.

Responsibility

People, according to Gestalt therapy, are responsible (response-able); that is, they are the primary agents in determining their own behavior. When people confuse responsibility with blaming and shoulds, they pressure and manipulate themselves; they "try" and are not integrated and spontaneous. In such instances their true wants, needs and responses to the environment and choices in the situation are ignored and they overcomply or rebel against shoulds.

Gestalt therapists believe in the importance of a clear distinction between what one chooses and what is given. People are responsible for what they choose to do. For example, people are responsible for their actions on behalf of the environment. Blaming outside forces (e.g., genetics or parents) for what one chooses is self-deception. Taking responsibility for what one did not choose, a typical shame reaction, is also a deception. People are responsible for moral choices. Gestalt therapy helps patients discover what is moral according to their own choice and values. Far from advocating "anything goes," Gestalt therapy places a most serious obligation on each person: choosing and valuing.

Variety of Concepts

Gestalt therapy personality theory has evolved primarily out of clinical experience. The focus has been a theory of personality that supports our task as psychotherapists rather than an overall theory of personality. The constructs of Gestalt therapy theory are field theoretical rather than genetic and phenomenological rather than conceptual.

Although Gestalt therapy is phenomenological, it also deals with the unconscious, that is, with what does not enter into awareness when needed.

In Gestalt therapy, awareness is conceived of as being in touch and unawareness as being out of touch. Unawareness can be explained by a variety of phenomena, including learning what to attend to, repression, cognitive set, character and style. Simkin compared personality to a floating ball -- at any given moment only a portion is exposed while the rest is submerged. Unawareness is the result of the organism's not being in touch with its external environment due to its being mostly submerged in its own internal environment or fantasies, or not being in touch with its inner life due to fixation on the external.

Gestalt Therapy Theory of Change

Children swallow whole (introject) ideas and behavior. This results in an enforced morality rather than an organismically compatible morality. As a result, people frequently feel guilt when they behave in accordance with their wants as opposed to their shoulds. Some people invest an enormous amount of energy in maintaining the split between shoulds and wants -- the resolution of which requires a recognition of their own morality as opposed to an introjected one. Shoulds sabotage such people, and the more they push to be what they are not, the more resistance is set up, and no change occurs.

Beisser advanced the theory that change does not happen through a "coercive attempt by the individual or by another person to change him," but does happen if the person puts in the time and effort to be "what he is," "to be fully in his current position". When the therapist rejects the change agent role, change that is orderly and also meaningful is possible. The Gestalt therapy notion is that awareness (including owning, choice, and responsibility) and contact bring natural and spontaneous change. Forced change is an attempt to actualise an image rather than to actualise the self. With awareness self-acceptance, and the right to exist as is, the organism can grow. Forced intervention retards this process.

The Gestalt psychology principle of Prägnanz states that the field will form itself into the best Gestalt that global conditions will allow. So, too, Gestalt therapists believe that people have an innate drive to health. This propensity is found in nature, and people are part of nature. Awareness of the obvious, the awareness continuum, is a tool that a person can deliberately use to channel this spontaneous drive for health.

Polarities versus Dichotomies

A dichotomy is a split whereby the field is considered not as a whole differentiated into different and interlocking parts, but rather as an assortment of competing (either/or) and unrelated forces. Dichotomous thinking interferes with organismic self-regulation. Dichotomous thinking tends to be intolerant of diversity among persons and of paradoxical truths about a single person.

Organismic self-regulation leads to integrating parts with each other and into a whole that encompasses the parts. The field is often differentiated into polarities: parts that are opposites that complement or explicate each other. The positive and negative poles of an electrical field are the prototypical mode for this differentiation in a field theoretical way. The concept of polarities treats opposites as part of one whole, as yin and yang.

With this polar view of the field, differences are accepted and integrated. Lack of genuine integration creates splits, such as body-mind, self-external, infantile-mature, biological-cultural, and unconscious-conscious. Through dialogue there can be an integration of parts, into a new whole in which there is a differentiated unity. Dichotomies such as the self-ideal and the needy self, thought and impulse, and social requirements and personal needs can be healed by integrating into a whole differentiated into natural polarities.

Clarity of Gestalt

The good Gestalt describes a perceptual field organised with clarity and good form. A well-formed figure clearly stands out against a broader and less distinct background. The relation between that which stands out (figure) and the context (ground) is meaning. In the good Gestalt the meaning is clear. The good Gestalt gives a content-free definition of health.

In health, the figure changes as needed, that is, it shifts to another focus when the need is met or superseded by a more urgent need. It does not change so rapidly as to prevent satisfaction (as in hysteria) or so slowly that new figures have no room to assume organismic dominance (as in compulsivity). When figure and ground are dichotomised, one is left with a figure out of context or a context without focus. In health, awareness accurately represents the dominant need of the whole field. Need is a function of external factors (physical structure of the field, political activity, acts of nature, and so on) and internal factors (hunger, fatigue, interest, past experience, and so forth).

Polarity of Creative Adjustment

The Gestalt therapy concept of healthy functioning includes creative adjustment. A psychotherapy that only helps patients adjust creates conformity and stereotypy. A psychotherapy that only led people to impose themselves on the world without considering others would engender pathological narcissism and a world-denying realisation of self isolated from the world.

A person who shows creative interaction takes responsibility for the ecological balance between self and surroundings. This is the theoretical context within which some seemingly individualistic and even anarchistic statements of Gestalt therapy are most accurately considered. The individual and environment form a polarity. The choice is not between the individual and society, but between organismic and arbitrary regulation.

Resistance is a part of a polarity consisting of an impulse and resistance to that impulse. Seen as a dichotomy, resistance is often treated as "bad" and, in such a context, often turns out to be nothing more than the patient's following personal dictates rather than the therapist's. Seen as a polarity, resistance is as integral to health as the trait's being resisted.

Gestalt therapists attend to both the working process of consciousness and the resistance process of consciousness. Many Gestalt therapists avoid the word resistance because of its pejorative dichotomised connotation, which frames the process as a power battle between therapist and patient rather than as the self-conflict of the patient that needs to be integrated into a harmoniously differentiated self.

Impasse

An impasse is a situation in which external support is not

forthcoming and the person believes he cannot support himself. The latter is due in large part to the person's strength being divided between impulse and resistance. The most frequent method of coping with this is to manipulate others. An organismically self-regulating person takes responsibility for what is done for self, what is done by others for self, and what is done for others by self. The person exchanges with the environment, but the basic support for regulation of one's existence is by self.

When the individual does not know this, external support becomes a replacement for self-support rather than a source of nourishment for the self. In most psychotherapy the impasse is circumvented by external support by the therapist, and the patient does not find that self-support is sufficient. In Gestalt therapy, patients can get through the impasse because of the emphasis on loving contact without doing the patient's work, that is, without rescuing or infantilising.

Theory of Psychotherapy

In Gestalt, the only goal is awareness. This includes greater awareness in a particular area and also greater ability for the patient to bring automatic habits into awareness as needed. In the former sense awareness is a content, in the latter sense it is a process. Both awareness as content and awareness as process progress to deeper levels as the therapy proceeds. Awareness includes knowing the environment, responsibility for choices, self-knowledge, and self-acceptance, and the ability to contact.

Beginning patients are chiefly concerned with the solution of problems. The issue for the Gestalt therapist is how patients support themselves in solving problems.

Gestalt therapy facilitates problem solving through increased self-regulation and self-support by the patient. As therapy goes on, the patient and the therapist turn more attention to general personality issues. By the end of successful therapy the patient directs much of the work and is able to integrate problem solving, characterological themes, relationship issues with the therapist, and means of regulating his or her own awareness.

Gestalt therapy is most useful for patients open to working on self-awareness and for those who want natural mastery of their awareness process. Although some people claim they are interested in changing their behavior, most people seeking psychotherapy mainly want relief from discomfort. Their complaint may be generalised malaise, specific discomforts, or dissatisfaction in relationships. Patients often expect that relief will result from their therapist's doing the work rather than from their own efforts.

Psychotherapy is most appropriate for persons who create anxiety, depression, and so forth by rejecting themselves, alienating aspects of themselves, and deceiving themselves. In short, people who do not know how they further their own unhappiness are prime candidates, providing they are open to awareness work, especially awareness of self-regulation. Gestalt therapy is especially appropriate for those who know intellectually about themselves and yet don't grow.

Those who want symptom relief without doing awareness work may be better candidates for behavior modification, medication, biofeedback, and so on. The direct methods of Gestalt therapy facilitate patients' making this choice early in the therapy. However, patients' difficulty in doing the contact or awareness work should not automatically be interpreted as meaning that they do not want to work. Respect for the total person enables a Gestalt therapist to help the patients become clear about the differences between "can't" and "won't" and to know how internal barriers or resistance, such as prior learning, anxiety, shame and sensitivity to narcissistic injury, inhibit awareness work.

No "Shoulds"

There are no "shoulds" in Gestalt therapy. In Gestalt therapy a higher value is placed on the autonomy and the self-determination for the patient than on other values. This is not a should, but a preference. The no-should ethic takes precedence over the therapist's goals for the patient and leaves the responsibility and sanctioning of the patient's behavior to the patient.

Gestalt therapy is an exploration rather than a direct modification of behavior. The goal is growth and autonomy through an increase in consciousness. Rather than maintaining distance and interpreting, the Gestalt therapist meets patients and guides active awareness work. The therapist's active presence is alive and excited (hence warm), honest and direct. Patients can see, hear and be told how they are experienced, what is seen, how the therapist feels, what the therapist is like as a person.

Growth occurs from real contact between real people. Patients learn how they are seen and how their awareness process is limited, not primarily by talking about their problems, but by how they and the therapist engage each other. Focusing runs the range from simple inclusions or empathy to exercises arising mostly from the therapist's phenomenology while with the patient. Everything is secondary to the direct experience of both participants.

The general approach of Gestalt therapy is to facilitate exploring in ways that maximise what continues to develop after the session and without the therapist. The patient is often left unfinished but thoughtful or "opened up," or with an assignment. This is like a roast that continues to cook after being removed from the oven. This is in part how Gestalt therapy can be so intensive on fewer sessions per week. We cooperate with growth occurring without us; we initiate where needed.

Perls believed that the ultimate goal of psychotherapy was the achievement of "that amount of integration which facilitates its own development". An example of this kind of facilitation is the analogy of a small hole cut into an accumulation of snow. Once the draining process begins, the base that began as a small hole enlarges by itself. Successful psychotherapy achieves integration. Integration requires identification with all vital functions—not with only some of the patient's ideas, emotions and actions. Any rejection of one's own ideas, emotions or actions results in alienation.

Reowning allows the person to be whole. The task, then, in therapy is to have the person become aware of previously alienated parts and taste them, consider them and assimilate them if they are ego-syntonic or reject them if they prove to be ego-alien. Simkin has used the simile of a cake in encouraging patients to reown the parts of themselves that they have considered noxious or otherwise unacceptable: although the oil, or flour, or baking powder by themselves can be distasteful, they are indispensable to the success of the whole cake.

Gestalt therapy focuses on the patient, as any therapy does. However, the relationship is horizontal, thus differing from the traditional therapy relationship. In Gestalt therapy the therapist and patient speak the same language, the language of present centeredness, emphasising direct experience of both participants. Therapists as well as patients in Gestalt therapy show their full presence.

Since its beginning, Gestalt therapy has emphasised the patient's experience as well as the therapist's observation of what is not in the patient's awareness. This allows the patient to act as an equal who has full access to the data of his own experience so he can directly experience from inside what is observed by the therapist from outside. In an interpretive system the patient is an amateur and does not have the theoretical foundation for the interpretation. It is assumed that the important internal data are unconscious and not experienced.

An important aspect of the Gestalt therapy relationship is the question of responsibility. Gestalt therapy emphasises that both the therapist and the patient are self-responsible. When therapists regard themselves as responsible for patients, they collude with patients' not feeling self-responsible and thereby reinforce the necessity for manipulation due to the belief that patients are unable to support and regulate themselves. However, it is not enough for the therapist to be responsible for self and for the patient to be responsible for self -- there is also an alliance of patient and therapist that must be carefully constantly, and competently attended to.

Therapists are responsible for the quality and quantity of their presence, for knowledge about themselves and the patient, for maintaining a nondefensive posture, and for keeping their awareness and contact processes clear and matched to the patient. They are responsible for the consequences of their own behavior and for establishing and maintaining the therapeutic atmosphere.

In Gestalt therapy there is a constant and careful emphasis on what the patient does and how it is done. What does the patient face? How does the patient make choices? Does the patient self-support or resist?

Direct experience is the tool, and it is expanded beyond what is at first experienced by continuing to focus deeper and broader. The techniques of Gestalt therapy are experimental tasks. They are the means of expanding direct experience. These are not designed to get the patient somewhere, to change the patient's feelings, to recondition, or to foster catharsis.

In a phenomenological therapy "now" starts with the present awareness of the patient. What happens first is not childhood, but what is experienced now. Awareness takes place now. Prior events may be the object of present awareness, but the awareness process (e.g., remembering) is now. Not knowing the present, not remembering, or not anticipating are all disturbances.

The present is an ever-moving transition between the past and future. Frequently patients do not know their current behavior In some cases patients live in the present as if they had no past. Most patients live in the future as if it were now. All these are disturbances of time awareness.

In the therapy hour, when the patients refer to their lives out of the hour, or earlier in the hour, that is not now. In Gestalt therapy we orient more to the now than in any other form of psychotherapy. Experiences of the past few minutes, days, years or decades that are of present importance are dealt with. We attempt to move from talking about to directly experiencing. For example, talking to a person who is not physically present rather than talking about that person mobilises more direct experience of feelings.

Process of Psychotherapy

Gestalt therapy probably has a greater range of styles and modalities than any other system. It is practiced in individual therapy, groups, workshops, couples, families, and with children. It is practiced in clinics, family service agencies, hospitals, private practices, growth centers, and so on. The styles in each modality vary drastically on many dimensions: degree and type of structure; quantity and quality of techniques used; frequency of sessions; abrasiveness-ease of relating; focus on body, cognition, feelings, interpersonal contact; knowledge of and work with psychodynamic themes; degree of personal encountering, and so forth.

All styles and modalities of Gestalt therapy have in common the general principles we have been discussing: emphasis on direct experience and experimenting (phenomenology), use of direct contact and personal presence (dialogic existentialism), and emphasis on the field concepts of what and how and here and now. Within these parameters, interventions are patterned according to the context and the personalities of the therapist and the patient.

At the heart of the methodology is the emphasis on the difference between "work" and other activities, especially "talking about." Work has two meanings. First, it refers to a deliberate, voluntary and disciplined commitment to use phenomenologically focused awareness to increase the scope and clarity of one's life. When one moves from talking about a problem or being with someone in a general way to studying what one is doing, especially being aware of how one is aware, one is working. Second, in a group, work means being the primary focus of the therapist's and/or the group's attention.

Differences in techniques are not important, although the quality and type of therapeutic contact and a fit between the attitude and emphasis of the therapist and the patient's needs are important. Techniques are just techniques: the overall method, relationship, and attitude are the vital aspects. Nevertheless a discussion of some techniques or tactics might elucidate the overall methodology. These are only illustrative of what is possible.

Techniques of Patient Focusing

All techniques of patient focusing are elaborations of the question, "What are you aware of (experiencing) now?" and the instruction, "Try this experiment and see what you become aware of (experience) or learn." Many interventions are as simple as asking what the patient is aware of, or more narrowly, "What are you feeling?" or "What are you thinking?"

"Stay with it." A frequent technique is to follow an awareness report with the instruction: "Stay with it" or "Feel it out." "Stay with it" encourages the patient to continue with the feeling that is being reported, which builds the patient's capacity to deepen and work a feeling through to completion.

Enactment. Here the patient is asked to put feelings or thoughts into action. For example, the therapist may encourage the patient to "say it to the person" (if present) or use some kind of role playing (such as speaking to an empty chair if the person is not present). "Put words to it" is another example. The patient with tears in his eyes might be asked to "put words to it." Enactment is intended as a way of increasing awareness, not as a form of catharsis. It is not a universal remedy.

Exaggeration is a special form of enactment. A person is asked to exaggerate some feeling, thought, movement, etc., in order to feel the more intense (albeit artificial) enacted or fantasied vision. Enactment into movement, sound, art, poetry, etc., can both stimulate creativity and be therapeutic. For instance, a man who had been talking about his mother without showing any special emotion was asked to describe her. Out of his description came the suggestion to move like her. As the patient adopted her posture and movement, intense feelings came back into his awareness.

Guided fantasy. Sometimes a patient can bring an experience into the here and now more efficiently by visualising than by enacting:

This patient became aware of how he created his own anxiety and impotence. This fantasy was recreating an event that happened in order to get in better touch with it. The fantasy could be of an expected event, a metaphorical event, and so forth. In another case, a patient working on shame and self-rejection is asked to imagine a mother who says and means "I love you just the way you are." As the fantasy is given detail, the patient attends to her experience. This fantasy helps the patient become aware for the possibility of good self-mothering and can serve as a transition to integrate good self-parenting. The image can be used to work between sessions or as a meditation. It also raises feelings about experiences with abandonment, loss and bad parenting.

Loosening and integrating techniques. Often the patient is so fettered by the bonds of the usual ways of thinking that alternative possibilities are not allowed into awareness. This includes traditional mechanisms, such as denial or repression, but also cultural and learning factors affecting the patient's way of thinking. One technique is just to ask the patient to imagine the opposite of whatever is believed to be true.

Integrating techniques bring together processes the patient doesn't bring together or actively keeps apart (splitting). The patient might be asked to put words to a negative process, such as tensing, crying or twitching. Or when the patient verbally reports a feeling, that is, an emotion, she might be asked to locate it in her body. Another example is asking a patient to express positive and negative feelings about the same person.

Body techniques. These include any technique that brings patients' awareness to their body functioning or helps them to be aware of how they can use their bodies to support excitement, awareness and contact.

Therapist Disclosures

The Gestalt therapist is encouraged to make "I" statements. Such statements facilitate both the therapeutic contact and the patient's focusing and are to be made discriminatingly and judiciously. Using the "I" to facilitate therapeutic work requires technical skill, personal wisdom and self-awareness on the therapist's part. Therapists may share what they see, hear or smell. They can share how they are affected. Facts of which the therapist is aware and the patient is not are shared, especially if the information is unlikely to be spontaneously discovered in the phenomenological work during the hour, yet is believed to be important to the patient.

New Psychotherapy Mechanisms

The child needs a parental relationship with a nurturant,

organismic/environmental, ecological balance. For example, a mother must see that a child's needs are met and that the development of its potentialities are facilitated. A child needs this warm, nurturing kind of mirroring. And a child also needs room to struggle, to be frustrated, and to fail. A child also needs limits to experience the consequences of behavior. When parents cannot meet these needs because they need a dependent child or lack sufficient inner resources, the child develops distorted contact boundaries, awareness and lowered self-esteem.

Unfortunately, children are often shaped to meet the approval of parents on their own needs. As a result, the spontaneous personality is superseded by an artificial one. Other children come to believe they can have their own needs met by others without consideration for the autonomy of others. This results in the formation of impulsivity rather than spontaneity. Patients need a therapist who will relate in a healthy, contactful manner, neither losing self by indulgent the patient at the expense of exploration and working through nor creating excessive anxiety, shame and frustration by not being respectful, warm, receptive, direct and honest.

Patients who enter psychotherapy with decreased awareness of their needs and strengths, resisting rather than supporting their organismic self, are in pain. They try to get the therapist to do for them what they believe they cannot do for themselves. When therapists go along with this, patients do not reown and integrate their lost or never-developed potential. Therefore they still cannot operate with organismic self-regulation, being responsible for themselves. They do not find out if they have the strength to exist autonomously because the therapist meets their needs without strengthening their awareness and ego boundaries.

As Gestalt therapy proceeds and patients learn to be aware and responsible and contactful, their ego functioning improves. As a result, they gain tools for deeper exploration. The childhood experiences of the formative years can then be explored without the regression and overdependency necessary in regressive treatment and without the temporary loss of competence that a transference neurosis entails. Childhood experiences are brought into present awareness without the assumption that patients are determined by past events. Patients actively project transference material on the Gestalt therapist, thereby giving opportunities for deeper exploration.

Frustration and Support

Gestalt therapy balances frustration and support. The therapist explores rather than gratifies the patient's wishes -- and this is frustrating for the patient. Providing contact is supportive, although honest contact frustrates manipulation. The Gestalt therapist expresses self and emphasises exploring, including exploring desire, frustration and indulgence. The therapist responds to manipulations by the patient without reinforcing them, without judging and without being purposely frustrating. A balance of warmth and firmness is important.

Paradoxical Theory of Change

The paradox is that the more one tries to be who one is not, the more one stays the same. Many patients focus on what they "should be" and at the same time resist these shoulds. The Gestalt therapist attempts to work toward integration by asking the client to identify with each conflicting role. The client is asked what he or she experiences at each moment. When the client can be aware of both roles, integrating techniques are used to transcend the dichotomy.

There are two axioms in Gestalt therapy: "What is, is," and "One thing leads to another". The medium of change is a relationship with a therapist who makes contact based on showing who he or she truly is and who understands and accepts the patient. Awareness of "what is" leads to spontaneous change. When the person manipulating for support finds a therapist who is contactful and accepting and who does not collude with the manipulation, he may become aware of what he is doing. This Aha! is a new gestalt, a new outlook, a taste of new possibility: "I can be with someone and not manipulate or be manipulated." When such a person meets "therapeutic" collusion, derision, mind games, game busting and so on, this increase in awareness is unlikely to happen.

At each and every point along the way this new Aha! can occur. As long as the therapist or the patient can see new possibilities and the patient wants to learn, new Aha!'s are possible and with them, growth. Awareness work can start anywhere the patient is willing, if the therapist is aware and connects it to the whole. The ensuing process in Gestalt therapy leads to changes everywhere in the field. The more thorough the investigation, the more intense the reorganisation. Some changes can only be appreciated years later.

Patients in Gestalt therapy are in charge of their lives. The therapist facilitates attention to opening restricted awareness and areas of constricted contact boundaries; the therapist brings firmness and limits to areas with poor boundaries. As sensing increases in accuracy and vividness, as breathing becomes fuller and more relaxed and as patients make better contact, they bring the skills of therapy into their lives. Sometimes intimacy and job improvements follow Gestalt work like an act of grace, without the patient's connecting the increase to the work done in therapy. But the organism does grow with awareness and contact. One thing does lead to another.

Applications Problems

Gestalt therapy can be used effectively with any patient population that the therapist understands and feels comfortable with. If the therapist can relate to the patient, the Gestalt therapy principles of dialogue and direct experiencing can be applied. With each patient, general principles must be adapted to the particular clinical situation. If the patient's treatment is made to conform to "Gestalt therapy," it can be ineffective or harmful. A schisophrenic, a sociopath, a borderline and an obsessive-compulsive neurotic may all need different approaches. Thus, the competent practice of Gestalt therapy requires a background in more than Gestalt therapy. A knowledge of diagnosis, personality theory and psychodynamic theory is also needed.

The individual clinician has a great deal of discretion in Gestalt therapy. Modifications are made by the individual therapist according to the therapeutic style, personality, diagnostic considerations, and so on. This encourages and requires individual responsibility by the therapist. Gestalt therapists are encouraged to have a firm grounding in personality theory, psychopathology and theories and applications of psychotherapy, as well as adequate clinical experience. Participants in the therapeutic encounter are encouraged to experiment with new behavior and then share cognitively and emotionally what the experience was like.

Gestalt therapy has traditionally been considered most effective with "overly socialised, restrained, constricted individuals" (anxious, perfectionistic, phobic and depressed clients), whose inconsistent or restricted functioning is primarily a result of "internal restrictions". Such individuals usually show only a minimal enjoyment of living. Although Shepherd's statement accurately delineates a population Gestalt therapy is effective with, current clinical practice of Gestalt therapy includes treatment of a much wider range of problems.

Work with psychotic, disorganised, or otherwise severely disturbed people is more difficult and calls for "caution, sensitivity and patience." Shepherd advises against doing such work where it is not feasible to make a "long-term commitment" to the patient. Disturbed patients need support from the therapist and at least a minimal amount of faith in their own natural healing capacity before they can explore deeply and experience intensely the "overwhelming pain, hurt, rage and despair" that underlie the psychological processes of disturbed patients.

Working with more disturbed populations requires clinical knowledge of how to balance support and frustration, knowledge of character dynamics, need for auxiliary support (such as day treatment and medication) and so forth. Some statements which seem to make sense in a workshop encounter are obvious nonsense when applied in a broader context.

Gestalt therapy has been successfully employed in the treatment of a wide range of "psychosomatic" disorders including migraine, ulcerative colitis and spastic neck and back. Gestalt therapists have successfully worked with couples, with individuals having difficulties coping with authority figures and with a wide range of intrapsychic conflicts. Gestalt therapy has been effectively employed with psychotics and severe character disorders.

Because of the impact of Gestalt therapy and the ease with which strong, frequently buried affective reactions can be reached, it is necessary to establish safety islands to which both the therapist and patient can comfortably return. It is also imperative for the therapist to stay with the patient until he or she is ready to return to these safety islands. For example, after an especially emotion laden experience, the patient may be encouraged to make visual, tactile or other contact with the therapist or with one or more group members and report the experience.

Another safety technique is to have the patient shuttle back and forth between making contact in the now with the therapist or group members and with the emotionally laden unfinished situation that the patient was experiencing then until all of the affect has been discharged and the unfinished situation worked through. The Gestalt therapy emphasis on personal responsibility, interpersonal contact and increased clarity of awareness of what is, could be of great value in meeting the problems of the present.

Treatment of Individual Gestalt Therapy

Although Gestalt therapy has acquired a reputation for being primarily applicable to groups, its mainstay is actually individual treatment. Gestalt therapy begins with the first contact. Ordinarily, assessment and screening are done as a part of the ongoing relationship rather than in a separate period of diagnostic testing and social history taking. The data for the assessment are obtained by beginning the work, for example, by therapeutic encounter. This assessment includes the patient's willingness and support for work within the Gestalt therapy framework, the match of patient and therapist, the usual professional diagnostic and characterological discriminations, decisions on frequency of sessions, the need for adjunctive treatment and the need for medical consultation.

An average frequency for sessions is once per week. Using the Gestalt methodology, an intensity equivalent to psychoanalysis can often be achieved at this frequency. Often individual therapy is combined with group therapy, workshops, conjoint or family therapy, movement therapy, meditation, or biofeedback training. Sometimes patients can utilise more frequent sessions, but often they need the interval to digest material and more frequent sessions may result in overreliance on the therapist. Frequency of sessions depends on how long the patient can go between sessions without loss of continuity, decompensation, or lesser forms of relapse.

Frequency of sessions varies from five times per weel to every other week. Meeting less frequently than ever week obviously diminishes intensity unless the patien attends a weekly group with the same therapist. More thar twice a week is ordinarily not indicated, except wi psychotics, and is definitely contraindicated with borderli personality disorders. All through the therapy patients encouraged and aided in doing the decision making fo themselves. When to start and stop, whether to do an exercise, what adjunctive therapies to use, and the like are all discussed with the therapist, but the competence and ultimate necessity for the patient to make these choices is supported.

Group Models

Gestalt therapy groups vary from one and one-half to three hours in length, with an average length of two hours. A typical two-hour group has up to 10 participants. Gestalt therapists usually experience maximal involvement with heterogeneous groups, with a balance of men and women. Participants need to be screened. Any age is appropriate for Gestalt therapy, but an ongoing private practice group would typically range from ages 20 to 65 with the average between 30 and 50.

Some Gestalt therapists follow Perls' lead in doing one-on-one therapy in the group setting and use the "hot seat" structure. "According to this method, an individual expresses to the therapist his interest in dealing with a particular problem. The focus is then on the extended interaction between patient and group leader". One-on-one episodes average 20 minutes, but range from a couple of minutes to 45 minutes. During the one-on-one work, the other members remain silent. After the work, they give feedback on how they were affected, what they observed, and how their own experiences are similar to those the patient worked on. In recent years the one-on-one work has been expanded to include awareness work that is not focused around a particular problem.

Some observers have described the Gestalt therapist's style of group work as doing individual therapy in a group setting. This statement is valid for those Gestalt therapists who use the model just discussed and do not emphasise or deal with group dynamics or strive for group cohesiveness. However, this is only one style of Gestalt therapy—many Gestalt therapists do emphasise group dynamics.

Greater use of the group is certainly within the Gestalt methodology and is increasingly used in Gestalt therapy. This includes greater involvement of group members when an individual is doing one-on-one work, working on individual themes by everyone in the group, emphasis on interrelationships (contact) in the group, and working with group processes per se. The varied degree and type of structure provided by the leader include structured group exercises or no structured group exercises, observing the group's evolving to its own structure, encouraging one-on-one work, and so on.

Often Gestalt groups begin with some exercise to help participants make the transition into working by sharing here-and-now experience.

A frequently used model is one that encourages both increased awareness through focus on contact between group members and one-on-one work in the group (with other members encouraged to participate during the work). This encourages greater fluidity and flexibility.

Workshop Style

Some Gestalt therapy and a good deal of training in Gestalt therapy is conducted in workshops, which are scheduled for a finite period, some for as short as one day. Weekend workshops may ranged from 10 to 20 or more hours. Longer workshops range from a week through several months in duration. A typical weekend workshop membership consists of one Gestalt therapist and 12 to 16 people. Given longer periods (ranging from one week up to a month or longer), as many as 20 people can be seen by one therapist. Usually if the group is larger than 16 participants, co-therapists are used.

Because workshops have a finite life and because just so many hours are available to the participants, there is usually high motivation to "work." Sometimes, rules are established so that no one can work a second time until every other participant has had an opportunity to work once. At other times, no such rules are set. Thus, depending on their willingness, audacity and drive, some people may get intense therapeutic attention several times during a workshop.

Although some workshops are arranged with established groups, most assemble people for the first time. As in ongoing groups, the ideal practice is to screen patients before the workshop. An unscreened workshop requires a clinician experienced with the range of severe pathology and careful protection for possibly vulnerable group members. Confrontive or charismatic Gestalt styles are particularly likely to exacerbate existing mental illness in some participants.

14

Rational Emotive Behaviour Therapy (REBT)

Rational Emotive Behaviour Therapy (REBT) is an action-oriented therapeutic approach that stimulates emotional growth by teaching people to replace their self-defeating thoughts, feelings and actions with new and more effective ones. REBT teaches individuals to be responsible for their own emotions and gives them the power to change and overcome unhealthy behaviours that interfere with their ability to function and enjoy life, and is based on these simple principles:

— You are responsible for your own emotions and actions

— Your harmful emotions and dysfunctional behaviours are the product of your irrational thinking.

— You can learn more realistic views of the world and, with practice, make them a part of you.

— You can take charge of your irrational thoughts and change them to live a more productive and meaningful life.

Rational emotive behaviour therapy focuses on uncovering irrational beliefs which may lead to unhealthy negative emotions and replacing them with more productive rational alternatives.

Rational emotive behaviour therapy ('REBT') views human beings as 'responsibly hedonistic' in the sense that they strive to remain alive and to achieve some degree of happiness. However, it also holds that humans are prone to adopting irrational beliefs and behaviours which stand in the way of their achieving their goals and purposes. Often, these irrational attitudes or philosophies take the form of extreme or dogmatic 'musts', 'shoulds', or 'oughts'; they contrast with rational and flexible desires, wishes, preferences and wants. The presence of extreme philosophies can make all the difference between *healthy* negative emotions (such as sadness or regret or concern) and *unhealthy* negative emotions (such as depression or guilt or anxiety).

For example, one person's philosophy after experiencing a loss might take the form: "It is unfortunate that this loss has occurred, although there is no actual reason why it should not have occurred. Most importantly of all, REBT maintains that individuals have it within their power to change their beliefs and philosophies profoundly, and thereby to change radically their state of psychological health.

REBT employs the 'ABC framework' — depicted in the figure below — to clarify the relationship between activating events (A); our beliefs about them (B); and the cognitive, emotional or behavioural consequences of our beliefs (C). The ABC model is also used in some renditions of cognitive therapy or cognitive behavioural therapy, where it is also applied to clarify the role of mental activities or predispositions in mediating between experiences and emotional responses.

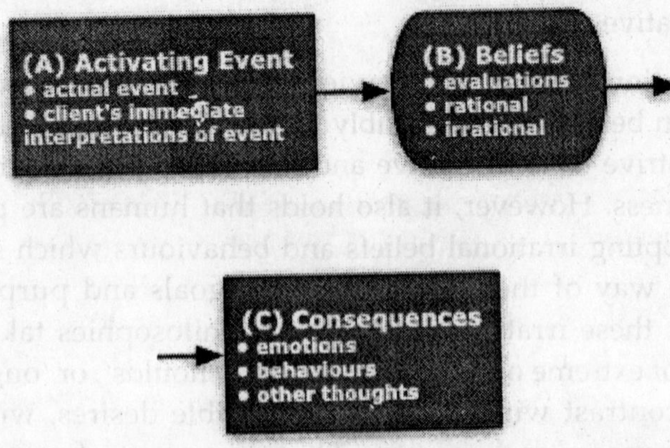

The figure below shows how the framework distinguishes between the effects of rational beliefs about negative events, which give rise to healthy negative emotions, and the effects of irrational beliefs about negative events, which lead to unhealthy negative emotions.

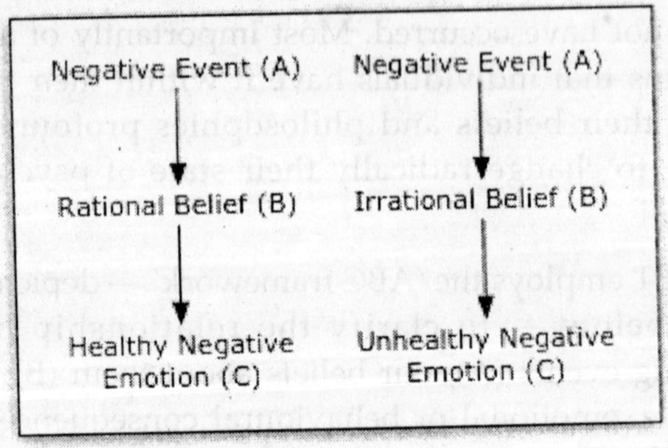

In addition to the ABC framework, REBT also employs three primary insights:

While external events are of undoubted influence, psychological disturbance is largely a matter of personal *choice* in the sense that individuals consciously or unconsciously *select* both rational beliefs and irrational beliefs at (B) when negative events occur at (A)

Past history and present life conditions strongly *affect* the person, but they do not, in and of themselves, *disturb* the person; rather, it is the individual's responses which disturb them, and it is again a matter of individual choice whether to maintain the philosophies at (B) which cause disturbance. Modifying the philosophies at (B) requires persistence and hard work, but it can be done.

Therapeutic Approach

The main purpose of REBT is to help clients to replace absolutist philosophies, full of 'musts' and 'shoulds', with more flexible ones; part of this includes learning to accept that all human beings (including themselves) are fallible and learning to increase their tolerance for frustration while aiming to achieve their goals.

Although emphasising the same 'core conditions' as person-centred counselling—namely, empathy, unconditional positive regard, and counsellor genuineness—in the counselling relationship, REBT views these conditions as neither necessary nor sufficient for therapeutic change to occur.

The basic process of change which REBT attempts to foster begins with the client acknowledging the existence of a problem and identifying any 'meta-disturbances' about that problem (i.e., problems about the problem, such as feeling guilty about being depressed). The client then identifies the underlying irrational belief which caused the original problem and comes to understand both why it is irrational and why a rational alternative would be preferable. The client challenges their irrational belief and employs a variety of cognitive, behavioural, emotive and imagery techniques to strengthen their conviction in a rational alternative. (For example, rational emotive imagery, or REI, helps clients practice changing unhealthy negative emotions into healthy ones at (C) while imagining the negative event at (A), as a way of changing their underlying philosophy at (B); this is designed to help clients move from an intellectual insight about which of their beliefs are rational and which irrational to a stronger 'gut' instinct about the same.) They identify impediments to progress and overcome them, and they work continuously to consolidate their gains and to prevent relapse.

To further this process, REBT advocates 'selective eclecticism', which means that REBT counsellors are encouraged to make use of techniques from other approaches, while still working specifically within the theoretical framework of REBT. In other words, REBT maintains theoretical coherence while pragmatically employing techniques that work.

Throughout, the counsellor may take a very directive role, actively disputing the client's irrational beliefs, agreeing homework assignments which help the client to overcome their irrational beliefs, and in general 'pushing' the client to challenge themselves and to accept the discomfort which may accompany the change process.

Rational Emotive Behaviour Therapy (REBT) for Suicidal Adolescents

Suicide is a leading cause of death among adolescents.

Admittedly, many would prefer not to talk about such a morbid topic, yet the realities are clear if one chooses to look at the statistics produced by the Center for Disease and Control (CDC). Suicide rates will continue to climb until more preventative programmes are developed.

Cognitive-Behavioural Therapies (CBT) are designed not only to reactively work with a suicidal adolescent, but more importantly, are structured to formulate work in a proactive manner. Nevertheless, a review of the literature is disappointing. Moreover, there was a paucity of research on the application of Rational Emotive Behaviour Therapy (REBT) and its application to suicidal adolescents.

Rational Emotive Behaviour Therapy (REBT) was developed and is still practiced by Albert Ellis. It is considered to be one the many cognitive-behavioural treatment modalities currently used in the mental health arena. The primary ingredients and major suppositions of REBT are similar to Beck's and Young's ideas and all of the other major cognitive behavioural thinkers' models; however, there are distinct differences within the REBT model, which deserve further exploration.

According to Ellis and Bernard, the difference between CBT and REBT "is that CBT does not attempt to modify the overall philosophy and assumptive world of clients through the use of disputational methods." Many of the CBT models seem to be more problem driven, while REBT appears to take the position that behaviour and/or emotions are simply consequences of the patient's core belief structure, which then leads to psychopathology.

According to the REBT model most commonly practiced, there are five key components a clinician must be familiar with. In an effort to be brief, the elements will be applied to a suicidal adolescent, while at the same time attempting to define each element. The acronym used by REBT therapists is the "ABCDE's" of REBT. "A" refers to the activating event. For example, an adolescent who is contemplating suicide or is simply thinking about suicide, the activating event could be as innocuous as a break up with a girl or boy friend, a poor grade on a test or simply an argument with a friend. "B" stands for the adolescent's rational or irrational belief about A.

For example, the adolescent may hold the cognition that because his girlfriend dumped him, he is "no longer loveable" and will be "incapable of having another relationship." Or, the belief may be more evaluative in nature, as he may be convinced that because of the breakup, "he is a bad person and a loser." One of the primary differences between REBT and other CBT models is the idea that the beliefs are not just irrational, but also evaluative in nature. Therefore, with a suicidal adolescent, it is imperative to not only identify the irrational beliefs, but also to determine the evaluative attributes of these beliefs. In this particular example, the irrational belief may be clear to the therapist; however, the "I am a loser because she dumped me" may not be as identifiable to the student. "C," according to Dryden, is the adolescent's behavioural and/ or emotional consequence of B (irrational beliefs).

Consistent with the example of the male adolescent being dumped by his girlfriend, he may become depressed, angry, or in this case suicidal. As a clinician, it is also imperative to be cognizant of the affective history of the student as well as the other risk factors associated with suicide. The clear advantage of REBT is the ability to link the displayed emotion to the belief and then to the activating event. With suicidal adolescents, the model is easy to understand and provides a linear model that is easy to understand by both the clinician and the student. "D" stands for disputation.

Disputation is a method of directly challenging the adolescent's irrational beliefs (B), by requesting for empirical evidence that he is a loser or he will be unable to have another relationship. Inherent within disputation is the idea of pragmatic empiricism. Here the therapist attempts to help the adolescent identify his irrationality surrounding the breakup as well as the idea of killing himself. The term "pragmatic," is direct and easy to comprehend, which is especially important for children and/or adolescents. For example, the therapist may ask the adolescent what evidence exists that suggests he is a loser. In addition, disputing the act of suicide would be paramount in this particular circumstance.

A possible method of disputing the idea of suicide would be to employ a didactic disputation strategy. According to Walden et al., "a second set of cognitive disputation strategies are didactic, including the use of mini-lectures, analogies, and parables. Some other possible methods of disputing suicidal ideation may be to ask how he would develop further relationships if he were dead. Additionally, why does he need to have a relationship with this girl if she is so "stupid" to dump him? It would be important to point out that suicide is an irrational response to a common adolescent problem and that there are many other methods of releasing or displaying his anger and/or sadness.

Disputation is unique to REBT and appears to be responsible for subsequent behavioural/affective/cognitive change. It differs from Beck's Socratic questioning, as it is more direct, easier to follow and more developmentally appropriate for adolescents. As Albert Ellis stated, "...other forms of therapy may help them feel better, but not get better. The goal is to get better rather than feel better. This is the goal of REBT." The utilisation of disputation is particularly important in this instance, as hopelessness can be easily disputed.

According to Jamison, "in short, when people are suicidal, their thinking is paralysed, their options appear spare or nonexistent, their mood is despairing, and hopelessness permeates their entire mental domain." Therefore, a possible disputation would be to point out to the adolescent that he is in fact hopeful and this particular event is simply a roadblock to bigger and better things. A therapist could empirically demonstrate to the adolescent that he would be missed if he decided to suicide by assembling a group of teachers, friends and family members who would corroborate the therapist's didactic disputation. These individuals could also confirm that he is likeable person who would be missed if he decided to kill himself.

Potential Strength of REBT

Some of the potential strengths of REBT and its application to suicidal youths would be its simplicity. REBT seems to be a model which takes into consideration, developmental levels—an important ingredient when working with teenagers. REBT, in some respect, may not seem like psychotherapy from the teenager's perspective, due to its direct approach, didactic style, and reliance on empiricism. Where other models of therapy come across as mysterious and intimidating to teenagers, REBT is exactly the opposite.

Another strength of REBT, particularly for adolescents, is its absence of moral and/or judgmental perspective. For example, if a teenager commits a crime, the expectation would be "you are a bad person." An REBT therapist, on the other hand, would most likely say, "you did commit a crime, yet this does not mean you are a bad person." This approach can be very reassuring to a teenager who is so accustomed to being judged for what they do, rather than for who they are.

According to Boyd and Grieger, "...RET is hypothesised to exceed the effectiveness of other cognitive-behavioural treatments by virtue of promoting unconditional self-acceptance and reducing 'secondary problems' such as self-criticism about having problems." Finally, REBT for an adolescent who may be contemplating suicide is logical, pragmatic and employs techniques which are developmentally congruent with the adolescent. While there are many potential strengths to REBT, unfortunately there do exist a few drawbacks.

Weinrach has indicated that REBT has the capability of rubbing individuals the wrong way. Another criticism, or to be more accurate, a misconception regarding REBT, is its failure to discuss the emotionality aspects of emotional disturbances. REBT has also been lambasted for being a model for tough-minded individuals. According to Ziegler, "...the counselling profession attracts primarily Tender-Minded students, people who are warm, sensitive, and caring. Tender-Minded counselling students are often threatened or alienated by a theory that espouses, life is often unfair."

Limitations of Rational Emotive Behaviour Therapy

As one leading proponent of REBT has indicated, REBT is easy to practise poorly, and it is from this that one immediate criticism suggests itself from the perspective of someone who takes a philosophical approach to life anyway: inelegant REBT could be profoundly irritating! The kind of conceptual disputing favoured by REBT could easily meander off track into minutiae relatively far removed from the client's central concern, and the mental gymnastics required to keep client and therapist on the same track could easily eat up time better spent on more productive activities. The counsellor's and client's estimations of relative importance could diverge rather profoundly, particularly if the client's outlook really does embody significant irrationalities. Having said all that, each of the preceeding sentences includes the qualifier *'could'*, and with a great deal of skill, each pitfall undoubtedly could be avoided.

Perhaps more importantly, it would appear that the need to match therapeutic approach with client preference is even more pressing with REBT than with many others. In other words, it seems very important to adopt the REBT approach only with clients who truly are suitable, as it otherwise risks being strongly counter-productive. On this point, however, it is crucial to realise that some clients specifically do appreciate *exactly* this kind of approach, and counsellors who are unable or unwilling to provide the disputation required are probably not right for those clients.

REBT is much less empirically supported than some other approaches: the requisite studies simply have not been completed yet, and the relevant data points for determining the best match with clients are therefore thin on the ground. However, one may envision clients responding particularly well who are both willing and able to conceptualise their problems within the ABC framework, and who are committed to active participation in the process of identifying and changing irrational beliefs (including performing homework assignments in support of the latter).

Clients will also need to be able to work collaboratively with a counsellor who will challenge and dispute with them directly, and a scientific and at least somewhat logical outlook would seem a pre-requisite. REBT would be less suitable for clients who do not meet one or more of the above. And as hinted above in the section on Criticims, one might also *speculate* that clients who are already highly skilled in philosophical engagement could find the approach less useful.

15

Hyperactivity Disorder

For many people, this is what it's like to have Attention Deficit Hyperactivity Disorder, or ADHD. They may be unable to sit still, plan ahead, finish tasks, or be fully aware of what's going on around them. To their family, classmates or coworkers, they seem to exist in a whirlwind of disorganised or frensied activity. Unexpectedly--on some days and in some situations--they seem fine, often leading others to think the person with ADHD can actually control these behaviours. As a result, the disorder can mar the person's relationships with others in addition to disrupting their daily life, consuming energy, and diminishing self-esteem.

ADHD, once called hyperkinesis or minimal brain dysfunction, is one of the most common mental disorders among children. It affects 3 to 5 percent of all children, perhaps as many as 2 million American children. Two to three times more boys than girls are affected. On the average, at least one child in every classroom in the United States needs help for the disorder. ADHD often continues into adolescence and adulthood, and can cause a lifetime of frustrated dreams and emotional pain.

Symptoms of ADHD

ADHD is not like a broken arm, or strep throat. Unlike these two disorders, ADHD does not have clear physical signs that can be seen in an x-ray or a lab test. Scientists have not yet identified a single cause behind all the different patterns of behaviour--and they may never find just one. Rather, someday scientists may find that ADHD is actually an umbrella term for several slightly different disorders.

At present, ADHD is a diagnosis applied to children and adults who consistently display certain characteristic behaviours over a period of time. The most common behaviours fall into three categories:

— inattention,

— hyperactivity, and

— impulsivity.

Inattention. People who are inattentive have a hard time keeping their mind on any one thing and may get bored with a task after only a few minutes. They may give effortless, automatic attention to activities and things they enjoy. But focusing deliberate, conscious attention to organising and completing a task or learning something new is difficult.

For example, Lisa found it agonising to do homework. Often, she forgot to plan ahead by writing down the assignment or bringing home the right books. And when trying to work, every few minutes she found her mind drifting to something else. As a result, she rarely finished and her work was full of errors.

Hyperactivity. People who are hyperactive always seem to be in motion. They can't sit still. Sitting still through a lesson can be an impossible task. Hyperactive children squirm in their seat or roam around the room. Or they might wiggle their feet, touch everything, or noisily tap their pencil. Hyperactive teens and adults may feel intensely restless.

Impulsivity. People who are overly impulsive seem unable to curb their immediate reactions or think before they act. Not everyone who is overly hyperactive, inattentive, or impulsive has an attention disorder. Since most people sometimes blurt out things they didn't mean to say, bounce from one task to another, or become disorganised and forgetful, how can specialists tell if the problem is ADHD?

To assess whether a person has ADHD, specialists consider several critical questions: Are these behaviours excessive, long-term, and pervasive? That is, do they occur more often than in other people the same age? Are they a continuous problem, not just a response to a temporary situation? Do the behaviours occur in several settings or only in one specific place like the playground or the office? The person's pattern of behaviour is compared against a set of criteria and characteristics of the disorder. These criteria appear in a diagnostic reference book called the DSM (short for the Diagnostic and Statistical Manual of Mental Disorders).

There are three patterns of behaviour that indicate ADHD. People with ADHD may show several signs of being consistently inattentive. They may have a pattern of being hyperactive and impulsive. Or they may show all three types of behaviour.

Some signs of hyperactivity and impulsivity are:

— feeling restless, often fidgeting with hands or feet, or squirming

— running, climbing, or leaving a seat, in situations where sitting or quiet behaviour is expected

— blurting out answers before hearing the whole question

— having difficulty waiting in line or for a turn

The behaviours must appear early in life, before age 7, and continue for at least 6 months. In children, they must be more frequent or severe than in others the same age. Above all, the behaviours must create a real handicap in at least two areas of a person's life, such as school, home, work, or social settings. So someone whose work or friendships are not impaired by these behaviours would not be diagnosed with ADHD. Nor would a child who seems overly active at school but functions well elsewhere.

The fact is, many things can produce these behaviours. Anything from chronic fear to mild seizures can make a child seem overactive, quarrelsome, impulsive, or inattentive. For example, a formerly cooperative child who becomes overactive and easily distracted after a parent's death is dealing with an emotional problem, not ADHD.

A chronic middle ear infection can also make a child seem distracted and uncooperative. So can living with family members who are physically abusive or addicted to drugs or alcohol. Can you imagine a child trying to focus on a math lesson when his or her safety and well-being are in danger each day? Such children are showing the effects of other problems, not ADHD.

In other children, ADHD-like behaviours may be their response to a defeating classroom situation. Perhaps the child has a learning disability and is not developmentally ready to learn to read and write at the time these are taught.

Or maybe the work is too hard or too easy, leaving the child frustrated or bored.

Tyrone and Mimi are two examples of how classroom conditions can elicit behaviours that look like ADHD. For months, Tyrone shouted answers out in class, then became disruptive when the teacher ignored him. He certainly seemed hyperactive and impulsive. Finally, after observing Tyrone in other situations, his teacher realised he just wanted approval for knowing the right answer. She began to seek opportunities to call on him and praise him. Gradually, Tyrone became calmer and more cooperative.

Mimi, a fourth grader, made loud noises during reading group that constantly disrupted the class. One day the teacher realised that the book was too hard for Mimi. Mimi's disruptions stopped when she was placed in a reading group where the books were easier and she could successfully participate in the lesson. Like Tyrone and Mimi, some children's attention and class participation improve when the class structure and lessons are adjusted a bit to meet their emotional needs, instructional level, or learning style. Although such children need a little help to get on track at school, they probably don't have ADHD.

It's also important to realise that during certain stages of development, the majority of children that age tend to be inattentive, hyperactive, or impulsive--but do not have ADHD. Preschoolers have lots of energy and run everywhere they go, but this doesn't mean they are hyperactive. And many teenagers go through a phase when they are messy, disorganised, and reject authority. It doesn't mean they will have a lifelong problem controlling their impulses.

ADHD is a serious diagnosis that may require long-term treatment with counselling and medication. So it's important that a doctor first look for and treat any other causes for these behaviours.

One of the difficulties in diagnosing ADHD is that it is often accompanied by other problems. For example, many children with ADHD also have a specific learning disability (LD), which means they have trouble mastering language or certain academic skills, typically reading and math. ADHD is not in itself a specific learning disability. But because it can interfere with concentration and attention, ADHD can make it doubly hard for a child with LD to do well in school.

A very small proportion of people with ADHD have a rare disorder called Tourette's syndrome. People with Tourette's have tics and other movements like eye blinks or facial twitches that they cannot control. Others may grimace, shrug, sniff, or bark out words. Fortunately, these behaviours can be controlled with medication. Researchers at NIMH and elsewhere are involved in evaluating the safety and effectiveness of treatment for people who have both Tourette's syndrome and ADHD.

More serious, nearly half of all children with ADHD--mostly boys--tend to have another condition, called oppositional defiant disorder. Who punched playmates for jostling him, these children may overreact or lash out when they feel bad about themselves. They may be stubborn, have outbursts of temper, or act belligerent or defiant. Sometimes this progresses to more serious conduct disorders. Children with this combination of problems are at risk of getting in trouble at school, and even with the police. They may take unsafe risks and break laws--they may steal, set fires, destroy property, and drive recklessly. It's important that children with these conditions receive help before the behaviours lead to more serious problems.

At some point, many children with ADHD--mostly younger children and boys--experience other emotional disorders. About one-fourth feel anxious. They feel tremendous worry, tension, or uneasiness, even when there's nothing to fear. Because the feelings are scarier, stronger, and more frequent than normal fears, they can affect the child's thinking and behaviour. Others experience depression.

Depression goes beyond ordinary sadness--people may feel so "down" that they feel hopeless and unable to deal with everyday tasks. Depression can disrupt sleep, appetite, and the ability to think. Because emotional disorders and attention disorders so often go hand in hand, every child who has ADHD should be checked for accompanying anxiety and depression. Anxiety and depression can be treated, and helping children handle such strong, painful feelings will help them cope with and overcome the effects of ADHD.

Of course, not all children with ADHD have an additional disorder. Nor do all people with learning disabilities, Tourette's syndrome, oppositional defiant disorder, conduct disorder, anxiety, or depression have ADHD. But when they do occur together, the combination of problems can seriously complicate a person's life. For this reason, it's important to watch for other disorders in children who have ADHD.

Causes of ADHD

Health professionals stress that since no one knows what causes ADHD, it doesn't help parents to look backward to search for possible reasons. There are too many possibilities to pin down the cause with certainty. It is far more important for the family to move forward in finding ways to get the right help.

Scientists, however, do need to study causes in an effort to identify better ways to treat, and perhaps some day, prevent ADHD. They are finding more and more evidence that ADHD does not stem from home environment, but from biological causes. When you think about it, there is no clear relationship between home life and ADHD. Not all children from unstable or dysfunctional homes have ADHD. And not all children with ADHD come from dysfunctional families. Knowing this can remove a huge burden of guilt from parents who might blame themselves for their child's behaviour.

Over the last decades, scientists have come up with possible theories about what causes ADHD. Some of these theories have led to dead ends, some to exciting new avenues of investigation. One disappointing theory was that all attention disorders and learning disabilities were caused by minor head injuries or undetectable damage to the brain, perhaps from early infection or complications at birth.

Based on this theory, for many years both disorders were called "minimal brain damage" or "minimal brain dysfunction." Although certain types of head injury can explain some cases of attention disorder, the theory was rejected because it could explain only a very small number of cases. Not everyone with ADHD or LD has a history of head trauma or birth complications.

Another theory was that refined sugar and food additives make children hyperactive and inattentive. As a result, parents were encouraged to stop serving children foods containing artificial flavourings, preservatives, and sugars. ADHD is not usually caused by:

— too much TV
— food allergies
— excess sugar
— poor home life
— poor schools

In recent years, as new tools and techniques for studying the brain have been developed, scientists have been able to test more theories about what causes ADHD. Adult subjects were asked to learn a list of words. As they did, scientists used a PET scanner to observe the brain at work. The researchers measured the level of glucose used by the areas of the brain that inhibit impulses and control attention. Glucose is the brain's main source of energy, so measuring how much is used is a good indicator of the brain's activity level. The investigators found important differences between people who have ADHD and those who don't.

In people with ADHD, the brain areas that control attention used less glucose, indicating that they were less active. It appears from this research that a lower level of activity in some parts of the brain may cause inattention. The next step will be to research WHY there is less activity in these areas of the brain. Scientists at NIMH hope to compare the use of glucose and the activity level in mild and severe cases of ADHD. They will also try to discover why some medications used to treat ADHD work better than others, and if the more effective medications increase activity in certain parts of the brain.

Researchers are also searching for other differences between those who have and do not have ADHD. Research on how the brain normally develops in the fetus offers some clues about what may disrupt the process. Throughout pregnancy and continuing into the first year of life, the brain is constantly developing. It begins its growth from a few all-purpose cells and evolves into a complex organ made of billions of specialised, interconnected nerve cells. By studying brain development in animals and humans, scientists are gaining a better understanding of how the brain works when the nerve cells are connected correctly and incorrectly. Scientists at NIMH and other research institutions are tracking clues to determine what might prevent nerve cells from forming the proper connections. Some of the factors they are studying include drug use during pregnancy, toxins, and genetics.

Research shows that a mother's use of cigarettes, alcohol, or other drugs during pregnancy may have damaging effects on the unborn child. These substances may be dangerous to the fetus's developing brain. It appears that alcohol and the nicotine in cigarettes may distort developing nerve cells. For example, heavy alcohol use during pregnancy has been linked to fetal alcohol syndrome (FAS), a condition that can lead to low birth weight, intellectual impairment, and certain physical defects. Many children born with FAS show much the same hyperactivity, inattention, and impulsivity as children with ADHD.

Drugs such as cocaine--including the smokable form known as crack--seem to affect the normal development of brain receptors. These brain cell parts help to transmit incoming signals from our skin, eyes, and ears, and help control our responses to the environment. Current research suggests that drug abuse may harm these receptors. Some scientists believe that such damage may lead to ADHD.

Toxins in the environment may also disrupt brain development or brain processes, which may lead to ADHD. Lead is one such possible toxin. It is found in dust, soil, and flaking paint in areas where leaded gasoline and paint were once used. It is also present in some water pipes. Some animal studies suggest that children exposed to lead may develop symptoms associated with ADHD, but only a few cases have actually been found.

Other research shows that attention disorders tend to run in families, so there are likely to be genetic influences. Children who have ADHD usually have at least one close relative who also has ADHD. And at least one-third of all fathers who had ADHD in their youth bear children who have ADHD. Even more convincing: the majority of identical twins share the trait. At the National Institutes of Health, researchers are also on the trail of a gene that may be involved in transmitting ADHD in a small number of families with a genetic thyroid disorder.

Diagnosis of ADHD

School-age and preschool children are often evaluated by a school psychologist or a team made up of the school psychologist and other specialists. But if the school doesn't believe the student has a problem, or if the family wants another opinion, a family may need to see a specialist in private practice.

The family can start by talking with the child's pediatrician or their family doctor. Some pediatricians may do the assessment themselves, but more often they refer the family to an appropriate specialist they know and trust. In addition, state and local agencies that serve families and children, as well as some of the volunteer organisations listed in the back of this booklet, can help identify an appropriate specialist.

Knowing the differences in qualifications and services can help the family choose someone who can best meet their needs. Besides school psychologists, there are several types of specialists qualified to diagnose and treat ADHD. Child psychiatrists are doctors who specialise in diagnosing and treating childhood mental and behavioural disorders. A psychiatrist can provide therapy and prescribe any needed medications.

Child psychologists are also qualified to diagnose and treat ADHD. They can provide therapy for the child and help the family develop ways to deal with the disorder. But psychologists are not medical doctors and must rely on the child's physician to do medical exams and prescribe medication. Neurologists, doctors who work with disorders of the brain and nervous system, can also diagnose ADHD and prescribe medicines. But unlike psychiatrists and psychologists, neurologists usually do not provide therapy for the emotional aspects of the disorder.

Adults who think they may have ADHD can also seek a psychologist, psychiatrist, or neurologist. But at present, not all specialists are skilled in identifying or treating ADHD in adults. Within each specialty, individual doctors and mental health professionals differ in their experience with ADHD. So in selecting a specialist, it's important to find someone with specific training and experience in diagnosing and treating the disorder.

Whatever the specialist's expertise, his or her first task is to gather information that will rule out other possible reasons for the child's behaviour. In ruling out other causes, the specialist checks the child's school and medical records. The specialist tries to sense whether the home and classroom environments are stressful or chaotic, and how the child's parents and teachers deal with the child. They may have a doctor look for such problems as emotional disorders, undetectable (petit mal) seisures, and poor vision or hearing.

Most schools automatically screen for vision and hearing, so this information is often already on record. A doctor may also look for allergies or nutrition problems like chronic "caffeine highs" that might make the child seem overly active. The child's teachers, past and present, are asked to rate their observations of the child's behaviour on standardised evaluation forms to compare the child behaviours to those of other children the same age. Of course, rating scales are subjective--they only capture the teacher's personal perception of the child. Even so, because teachers get to know so many children, their judgment of how a child compares to others is usually accurate.

The specialist interviews the child's teachers, parents, and other people who know the child well, such as school staff and baby-sitters. Parents are asked to describe their child's behaviour in a variety of situations. They may also fill out a rating scale to indicate how severe and frequent the behaviours seem to be. In some cases, the child may be checked for social adjustment and mental health. Tests of intelligence and learning achievement may be given to see if the child has a learning disability and whether the disabilities are in all or only certain parts of the school curriculum.

Adults are diagnosed for ADHD based on their performance at home and at work. When possible, their parents are asked to rate the person's behaviour as a child. A spouse or roommate can help rate and evaluate current behaviours. But for the most part, adults are asked to describe their own experiences. One symptom is a sense of frustration. Since people with ADHD are often bright and creative, they often report feeling frustrated that they're not living up to their potential. Many also feel restless and are easily bored. Some say they need to seek novelty and excitement to help channel the whirlwind in their minds. Although it may be impossible to document when these behaviours first started, most adults with ADHD can give examples of being inattentive, impulsive, overly active, impatient, and disorganised most of their lives.

Until recent years, adults were not thought to have ADHD, so many adults with ongoing symptoms have never been diagnosed. Psychotherapy and medication for anxiety, depression, or manic-depression fail to help much, simply because the ADHD itself is not being addressed. Yet half the children with ADHD continue to have symptoms through adulthood. The recent awareness of adult ADHD means that many people can finally be correctly diagnosed and treated.

A correct diagnosis lets people move forward in their lives. Once the disorder is known, they can begin to receive whatever combination of educational, medical, and emotional help they need. An effective treatment plan helps people with ADHD and their families at many levels. For adults with ADHD, the treatment plan may include medication, along with practical and emotional support. For children and adolescents, it may include providing an appropriate classroom setting, the right medication, and helping parents to manage their child's behaviour.

Educational Options

Children with ADHD have a variety of needs. Some children are too hyperactive or inattentive to function in a regular classroom, even with medication and a behaviour management plan. Such children may be placed in a special education class for all or part of the day. In some schools, the special education teacher teams with the classroom teacher to meet each child's unique needs. However, most children are able to stay in the regular classroom. Whenever possible, educators prefer to not to segregate children, but to let them learn along with their peers.

Children with ADHD often need some special accommodations to help them learn. For example, the teacher may seat the child in an area with few distractions, provide an area where the child can move around and release excess energy, or establish a clearly posted system of rules and reward appropriate behaviour. Sometimes just keeping a card or a picture on the desk can serve as a visual reminder to use the right school behaviour, like raising a hand instead of shouting out, or staying in a seat instead of wandering around the room.

Many of the strategies of special education are simply good teaching methods. Telling students in advance what they will learn, providing visual aids, and giving written as well as oral instructions are all ways to help students focus and remember the key parts of the lesson. Students with ADHD often need to learn techniques for monitoring and controlling their own attention and behaviour.

Although parents have the option of taking their child to a private practitioner for evaluation and educational services, most children with ADHD qualify for free services within the public schools. Steps are taken to ensure that each child with ADHD receives an education that meets his or her unique needs. For example, the special education teacher, working with parents, the school psychologist, school administrators, and the classroom teacher, must assess the child's strengths and weaknesses and design an

Individualised Educational Program (IEP). The IEP outlines the specific skills the child needs to develop as well as appropriate learning activities that build on the child's strengths. Parents play an important role in the process. They must be included in meetings and given an opportunity to review and approve their child's IEP.

Many children with ADHD or other disabilities are able to receive such special education services under the Individuals with Disabilities Education Act (IDEA). The Act guarantees appropriate services and a public education to children with disabilities from ages 3 to 21. Children who do not qualify for services under IDEA can receive help under an earlier law, the National Rehabilitation Act, Section 504, which defines disabilities more broadly. Qualifying for services under the National Rehabilitation Act is often called "504 eligibility." Because ADHD is a disability that affects children's ability to learn and interact with others, it can certainly be a disabling condition. Under one law or another, most children can receive the services they need.

Treatments to ADHD People

Life can be hard for children with ADHD. They're the ones who are so often in trouble at school, can't finish a game, and lose friends. They may spend agonising hours each night struggling to keep their mind on their homework, then forget to bring it to school. It's not easy coping with these frustrations day after day. Some children release their frustration by acting contrary, starting fights, or destroying property. Some turn the frustration into body ailments, like the child who gets a stomachache each day before school. Others hold their needs and fears inside, so that no one sees how badly they feel.

It's also difficult having a sister, brother, or classmate who gets angry, grabs your toys, and loses your things. Children who live with or share a classroom with a child who has ADHD get frustrated, too. They may feel neglected as their parents or teachers try to cope with the hyperactive child. They may resent their brother or sister never finishing chores, or being pushed around by a classmate. They want to love their sibling and get along with their classmate, but sometimes it's so hard!

It's especially hard being the parent of a child who is full of uncontrolled activity, leaves messes, throws tantrums, and doesn't listen or follow instructions. Parents often feel powerless and at a loss. The usual methods of discipline, like reasoning and scolding, don't work with this child, because the child doesn't really choose to act in these ways. It's just that their self-control comes and goes. Out of sheer frustration, parents sometimes find themselves spanking, ridiculing, or screaming at the child, even though they know it's not appropriate. Their response leaves everyone more upset than before. Then they blame themselves for not being better parents. Once children are diagnosed and receiving treatment, some of the emotional upset within the family may fade.

Medication can help to control some of the behaviour problems that may have lead to family turmoil. But more often, there are other aspects of the problem that medication can't touch. Even though ADHD primarily affects a person's behaviour, having the disorder has broad emotional repercussions. For some children, being scolded is the only attention they ever get. They have few experiences that build their sense of worth and competence. If they're hyperactive, they're often told they're bad and punished for being disruptive. If they are too disorganised and unfocused to complete tasks, others may call them lazy. If they impulsively grab toys, butt in, or shove classmates, they may lose friends. And if they have a related conduct disorder, they may get in trouble at school or with the law. Facing the daily frustrations that can come with having ADHD can make people fear that they are strange, abnormal, or stupid.

Often, the cycle of frustration, blame, and anger has gone on so long that it will take some time to undo. Both parents and their children may need special help to develop techniques for managing the patterns of behaviour. In such cases, mental health professionals can counsell the child and the family, helping them to develop new skills, attitudes, and ways of relating to each other. In individual counselling, the therapist helps children or adults with ADHD learn to feel better about themselves. They learn to recognise that having a disability does not reflect who they are as a person.

The therapist can also help people with ADHD identify and build on their strengths, cope with daily problems, and control their attention and aggression. In group counselling, people learn that they are not alone in their frustration and that others want to help. Sometimes only the individual with ADHD needs counselling support. But in many cases, because the problem affects the family as well as the person with ADHD, the entire family may need help. The therapist assists the family in finding better ways to handle the disruptive behaviours and promote change. If the child is young, most of the therapist's work is with the parents, teaching them techniques for coping with and improving their child's behaviour. Several intervention approaches are available and different therapists tend to prefer one approach or another. Knowing something about the various types of interventions makes it easier for families to choose a therapist that is right for their needs.

Psychotherapy works to help people with ADHD to like and accept themselves despite their disorder. In psychotherapy, patients talk with the therapist about upsetting thoughts and feelings, explore self-defeating patterns of behaviour, and learn alternative ways to handle their emotions. As they talk, the therapist tries to help them understand how they can change. However, people dealing with ADHD usually want to gain control of their symptomatic behaviours more directly. If so, more direct kinds of intervention are needed.

Cognitive-behavioural therapy helps people work on immediate issues. Rather than helping people understand their feelings and actions, it supports them directly in changing their behaviour. Social skills training can also help children learn new behaviours. In social skills training, the therapist discusses and models appropriate behaviours like waiting for a turn, sharing toys, asking for help, or responding to teasing, then gives children a chance to practice.

Support groups connect people who have common concerns. Many adults with ADHD and parents of children with ADHD find it useful to join a local or national support group. Many groups deal with issues of children's disorders, and even ADHD specifically. Members of support groups share frustrations and successes, referrals to qualified specialists, and information about what works, as well as their hopes for themselves and their children. There is strength in numbers--and sharing experiences with others who have similar problems helps people know that they aren't alone.

Parenting skills training, offered by therapists or in special classes, gives parents tools and techniques for managing their child's behaviour. One such technique is the use of "time out" when the child becomes too unruly or out of control. During time outs, the child is removed from the agitating situation and sits alone quietly for a short time to calm down. Parents may also be taught to give the child "quality time" each day, in which they share a pleasurable or relaxed activity. During this time together, the parent looks for opportunities to notice and point out what the child does well, and praise his or her strengths and abilities.

An effective way to modify a child's behaviour is through a system of rewards and penalties. The parents (or teacher) identify a few desirable behaviours that they want to encourage in the child--such as asking for a toy instead of grabbing it, or completing a simple task. The child is told exactly what is expected in order to earn the reward. The child receives the reward when he performs the desired behaviour and a mild penalty when he doesn't. A reward can be small, perhaps a token that can be exchanged for special privileges, but it should be something the child wants and is eager to earn. The penalty might be removal of a token or a brief "time out." The goal, over time, is to help children learn to control their own behaviour and to choose the more desired behaviour. The technique works well with all children, although children with ADHD may need more frequent rewards.

In addition, parents may learn to structure situations in ways that will allow their child to succeed. This may include allowing only one or two playmates at a time, so that their child doesn't get overstimulated. Or if their child has trouble completing tasks, they may learn to help the child divide a large task into small steps, then praise the child as each step is completed. Parents may also learn to use stress management methods, such as meditation, relaxation techniques, and exercise to increase their own tolerance for frustration, so that they can respond more calmly to their child's behaviour.

Controversial Treatments

Understandably, parents who are eager to help their children want to explore every possible option. Many newly touted treatments sound reasonable. Many even come with glowing reports. A few are pure quackery. Some are even developed by reputable doctors or specialists--but when tested scientifically, cannot be proven to help. Here are a few types of treatment that have not been scientifically shown to be effective in treating the majority of children or adults with ADHD:

— biofeedback
— restricted diets
— allergy treatments
— medicines to correct problems in the inner ear
— megavitamins
— chiropractic adjustment and bone re-alignment
— treatment for yeast infection
— eye training
— special coloured glasses

Group Counselling Intervention for Children with Attention Deficit Hyperactivity Disorder

Attention Deficit Hyperactivity Disorder (ADHD) is a

condition that becomes apparent in some children in the preschool and early school years. It is hard for these children to control their behaviour and/or pay attention. ADHD students often have problems in school where rules and procedures require them to sit still, be attentive, and stay focused on academic tasks and classroom discussions. They may receive some assistance from special education teachers who typically have smaller classes and who rely on the use of behavioural techniques in managing students.

In US, between 85% and 90% of ADHD students are still served in general education classrooms for all or part of the day. The regular classroom teacher works with a larger number of students at one time and usually lacks the training related to working with learning disorders. Some special education strategies may seem too impractical or time consuming, and many teachers are unsure of what to do and need support.

School counsellors, as behavioural and relationship specialists, can provide support for ADHD students and their teachers. The American School Counsellor Association published a position statement that strongly encourages the involvement of school counsellors in the multidimensional treatment of these students. Others in the field have also addressed the need. Counsellors provide such interventions as individual counselling, small group counselling, large group guidance, peer facilitator training, and consultation with parents, teachers, and administrators.

Sometimes certain student populations such as those with ADHD are targeted for special attention and one or more counsellor interventions. Braswell and Bloomquist recommend group counselling more often than individual counselling for most ADHD children. Group sessions closely approximate real-life peer relationship situations;

group members can help each other acquire skills and make generalisations.

Group counselling activities that elicit the behaviours and feelings associated with academic and social problems enable counsellors to intervene and assist children who are low performers in school and have difficulties with their peers. Interventions applied consistently within the school setting seem to be the most effective.

ADHD in Learning Environment

During the past decade, researchers linked the causes of ADHD to neurological and genetic factors. It appears that these factors may play a more important role than social or environmental ones, making the disorder a treatable but not necessarily curable one. This also suggests that the disorder might be managed but it is not likely to disappear. Barkley identified impulsivity as a hallmark of the disorder. Impulsive behaviour is also frequently seen in cases in which students are referred to school administrators for discipline. The greatest number of classroom problems and referrals associated with ADHD are related to behaviours that often cause conflicts with teachers and other students.

Counsellors want to help ADHD students gain the most from school by helping them manage their behaviour and adjust to rules and procedures. Although the onset of ADHD for most children is prior to age 4, it is most often diagnosed when a child is in elementary school. This is when children are introduced to the structure and demands of the educational system. How students learn to manage themselves and the learning environment during their first few years of school often determines how successful they will be in later years.

As many as 56% of ADHD students may require academic tutoring, up to 30% may repeat a grade, and 30% to 40% may be placed in special education programs. As many as 46% of ADHD students may be suspended from school with up to 35% dropping out completely and not finishing high school. In addition, without assistance students may develop emotional problems laden with anger, aggression, depression, and anxiety. These can lead to oppositional defiant and conduct disorders and result in troublesome conflicts.

Learning skills such as listening, attending, following directions, and exhibiting social competence have a strong correlation with successful social and academic achievement in school. Because ADHD students cannot sustain their attention and are easily distracted, they have difficulty doing academic tasks, completing homework, and acting appropriately with peers and teachers. Lack of success and repeated confrontations can lower self-esteem. Increased anxiety and frustration follow. Inconsistent performance in school, low test scores, disorganised desks and backpacks, and disruptive behaviour are additional problems that draw counsellors' attention.

ADHD Intervention

The most common treatment for ADHD is medication. Sixty percent to 90% of children diagnosed with the disorder receive stimulant medication for prolonged periods during their school careers. Short-term enhancements in behavioural functioning have been found in about 75% of those being treated with stimulant medication. Even though the medication has no effect on academic attainment per se, productivity in school may improve as a result of controlling behaviours that interfere with learning and classroom performance.

Stimulant medication does not teach appropriate behaviours, but it does increase the probability of a child displaying appropriate behaviours that are already in their repertoire. According to Barkley, the difficulty for ADHD students is not knowing what to do, but doing what they know. In addition, it has been shown that there is a difference between possessing a skill and using it effectively. An intervention that targets school success behaviours, including practice and application, increases the chances of improved behaviour for students who take stimulant medication.

Researchers Weiss & Hechtman, found the long-term prognosis for ADHD children treated with stimulant medication alone was the same as those receiving no treatment. A recent study sponsored by the National Institute of Mental Health reported that a carefully managed protocol of stimulant medication and behavioural intervention was effective in treating ADHD symptoms. The combination resulted in improved social skills, parent-child relations, and academic achievement. It was also reported that in some circumstances, behavioural/psychosocial interventions alone produced these same results. While school counsellors often help to identify behaviours symptomatic of ADHD, diagnosing and medically treating ADHD are not school counsellor functions. However, helping students understand and manage their behaviour and their relationships with others to maximise their learning potential is an important school counsellor function.

The widespread use of stimulant medication and the emphasis on behavioural modification by teachers and parents raises another question. Should ADHD students feel less responsibility for the outcomes of their behaviour? They may falsely conclude that what happens during the school day is the result of their medication and teachers' efforts, rather than their own choices and actions. This external locus of control can lead students to disclaim personal responsibility for what they do and lay a foundation for making excuses when problems or difficulties arise. Research findings support this external locus-of-control finding for ADHD students along with the need for explicit external cues.

However, Barkley suggests that ADHD is not an excuse or a reason to dismiss the consequences of one's actions, but rather an explanation as to why it is necessary for those with the disorder to increase awareness of life's behavioural contingencies. Helping students understand how their disorder affects school performance may be one way for ADHD students to begin to see themselves as having the capacity to manage themselves in their environment.

ADHD students need additional counsellor intervention strategies that (a) help them understand ADHD, (b) provide a repertoire of skills to enhance learning, and © help them understand the importance of external cues. Cognitive behavioural methods promote a shift from caregivers (teachers and parents) to the ADHD students themselves. The student is in the best position to recognise signs of problems before they occur and to take actions that help manage their lives.

Counselling Theory

Rational Emotive Behaviour Therapy (REBT) provides a theory for developing a group guidance unit that helps students learn how ADHD affects learning behaviours and classroom performance. It offers a rationale for increasing student awareness and the value of practicing school success skills. The theory assumes that an ADHD student cannot exhibit a behaviour that has not been learned.

REBT emphasises behavioural change and self-regulation along with the examination and possible modification of thoughts, beliefs, feelings, and expectations. It is an approach that supports recent treatment interventions for children with ADHD. It is assumed that, while the primary symptoms of the disorder are difficult to ameliorate, it may be possible to help children develop competencies that lower the risk of serious secondary difficulties.

Group Counselling Intervention

The intervention focuses on increased understanding of the disorder and how it impacts school performance. It was assumed that students needed to face their disorders and recognise that it is part of who they are. Further, the disorder by itself will not keep them from their personal, academic, or career goals. To the contrary, many individuals who have ADHD have made valuable and significant contributions to society. The secret to success is being able to manage one's thoughts, feelings, and behaviours.

Fourteen elementary school counsellors from one school district delivered the intervention consisting of six small group sessions designed for about six students per group. Each session had a specific objective related to thoughts, behaviours, and skills that focused on school and personal achievement and began with a review of the previous session and a check on application of skills. Sessions ended with tasks for practice and an encouraging summary statement. The unit culminated with snacks, juice, and talk about the group experience as well as a review of plans for utilising strategies. The sessions were based on the theme of a journey that students might imagine they were taking.

Of course, the journey required preparation and the ability to recognise certain road signs and to manage the vehicle in such a way that the students would arrive safely at their final destination. Because the students had ADHD, they would be a different kind of traveller and, at times, take a different route than others, although they would eventually arrive at the same destination. The metaphor of a journey provided opportunities to construct group activities that were fun and enabled participants to reflect on goals and goal setting, the influence of personal characteristics on achieving goals, and personal management skills. As they considered skills needed to move them along on their imaginary journey, they also thought about how the skills were related to the academic, personal, social, and career goals shared by all students their age.

Discussion and clarification help the students identify ADHD symptoms and how the symptoms are manifested in school, which often makes them learn in different ways than others. They are, in one sense, a different traveller in the education world. It is explained that sometimes they take the same road as others while learning things and then, at other times, they will go another way, perhaps taking some detours, even though everyone is trying to get to the same place. The counsellor leads the participants through a series of structured learning activities.

Special efforts are made to focus on what students experience (their feelings) and how those feelings are related to behaviours (their actions). Students discuss what they believe to be true about themselves and others, and how they can manage their thoughts, feelings, and behaviours.

16

Effective Group Counselling

In groups, individuals accomplish goals and relate to others in innovative and productive ways. People would not survive, let alone thrive, without involvement in groups. This reliance and interdependence is seen in all types of groups from those that are primarily task-oriented to those that are basically therapeutic. In order to be effective, group leaders must be aware of the power and potency of groups. They must plan ahead and they must be sensitive to the stage of development of the group. Equipped with this knowledge they can utilise appropriate skills to help their groups develop fully. Proper preparation and strategic intervention increase the chance of running a counselling group smoothly and effectively.

Effective Counselling Groups

A crucial element in starting counselling groups is making decisions beforehand. Pre-group planning is the first step in the process. Leaders design groups so that they will yield productive and pragmatic results for participants. Among the most important considerations are those associated with objectives, membership, rules, time, place, and dynamics.

Group counselling involves individuals who are having difficulties they wish to resolve that are of a personal, educational, social, or vocational nature. These groups are primarily run in educational institutions or agencies. They deal with specific, nonpathological problems that members are aware of prior to joining and which do not involve major personality changes. For instance, group counselling may focus on how members achieve such goals as relating better to their families, becoming organised, or relaxing in the presence of supervisors at work.

Group Membership

Group membership is either homogeneous or heterogeneous. Homogeneous groups are composed of individuals who are similar, such as adolescent boys, single parents or individuals working with grief and loss issues. Heterogeneous groups are made up of people who differ in background, such as adults of various ages with varied careers. While homogeneous groups can concentrate on resolving one issue, their members may be limited experientially. In contrast, heterogeneous groups offer diverse but multifocused membership.

Effective group leaders screen potential members before accepting them. Screening allows leaders to select members and members to select leaders and groups. The ideal group size of eight to 12 allows members an opportunity to express themselves without forming into subgroups. In order to help dispel and overcome misconceptions about groups, leaders can utilise pre-group interviews to identify fears related to upcoming groups. Through feedback and explanation, misunderstandings can be immediately clarified and corrected.

Rules and Regulations

Counselling groups run best when the rules governing them are few and clear. If there are more than a dozen rules, many members will tend to forget some of them. Likewise, if the rules are vague, some members will inevitably violate the letter or spirit of them. In counselling groups, rules should follow the ethical standards of professional organisations, such as the Association for Specialists in Group Work. Members should agree to keep each others' confidentiality, not attack each other verbally or physically, to actively participate in the group process, and to speak one at a time.

Time and Place

Although counselling groups vary, members need a specific, consistent time and place to meet. Most groups meet for one and one half to two hours each week for 12 to 16 sessions. The meeting room should be quiet and inviting and away from other activities. Groups work best when chairs are arranged in circles where everyone feels a sense of equality with one another and the flow of communication is enhanced.

Group Dynamics

Group member interactions appear simple but they are not. They are complex social processes that occur within groups and that affect actions and outcomes. Group dynamics occur in all groups, and involve the interactions of group members and leaders over time, including the roles the members and the leaders take. Individuals have an impact on groups just as groups influence members. The number of group interactions increases exponentially as the size of groups grows. Therefore, keeping track of communication patterns in counselling groups is a demanding job.

The complexity of interaction is magnified by the fact that messages are sent within counselling groups on a verbal as well as a nonverbal level. The nature of this communication is crucial to comprehending what is happening within groups. For example, a member who physically or emotionally distances from a group influences how the group operates as clearly as if he or she makes a statement. As groups develop, members frequently switch roles and patterns of interaction.

Stages of Groups

In addition to pre-planning, effective group counselling leaders recognise that groups go through five stages: dependency, conflict, cohesion, interdependence, and termination. The stages are often called forming, storming, norming, performing, and adjourning. Recognising group stages gives counsellors an opportunity to devise or utilise appropriate leadership interventions.

The first group stage is "dependency" or forming. At this time, group members are unsure of themselves and look to their leaders or others for direction. This process gives members an opportunity to explore who they are in the group and to begin establishing trust. The second stage in group counselling is "conflict," or storming. It may be overt or covert. The type and amount of conflict that is generated relates to how much jockeying for position goes on in the group. Stage three focuses on "cohesion," or norming, which can be defined as a spirit of "weness." In it, members become closer psychologically and are more relaxed. Everyone feels included in the group and productive sharing begins to occur.

In the fourth stage, performing, the main work of the group is begun. Interdependence develops. Group members are able to assume a wide variety of constructive roles and work on personal issues. The level of comfort in the group increases too. This is a prime time of problem solving. It occupies about 50% of a typical group's time. The final stage, adjourning deals with termination. Issues of loss in separating from the group are raised. Celebrating the accomplishment of goals is also a primary focus within this stage.

Effective Skills for Group Counselling

As with other groups, leaders of effective counselling groups need to employ a variety of interpersonal skills. Among the most important of these are:

a) active listening, where leaders are sensitive to the language, tone, and nonverbal gestures surrounding members' messages;

b) linking, where leaders help members recognise their similarities;

c) blocking, where leaders keep unfocused members from disrupting the group by either redirecting them or preventing them from monopolising conversation; and

d) summarising, where leaders help members become aware of what has occurred and how the group and its members have changed.

Empathy, personal warmth, courage, flexibility, inquiry, encouragement, and the ability to confront are vital skills too. Counselling group leaders must wear many hats in helping their groups make progress. The more skills within the counsellors' repertoires the more effective they will ultimately become.

Effective Counselling for Abused Children

Counselling abused children is a challenging task for practitioners. The incidence of reported and substantiated child abuse and neglect has risen dramatically since the "discovery" of the Battered Child Syndrome in the sixties, and subsequent mandatory reporting laws. Currently practitioners have become aware of the widespread sexual abuse of girls (estimated at one in four females) and are developing increasing awareness of the sexual abuse of boys. Rapid changes in the knowledge base demand that counsellors keep abreast of the indicators of maltreatment, the laws for reporting suspected abuse, and the ways in which children can best be served to overcome effects of a negative family experience.

All fifty states require that helping professionals report suspected child abuse to the child protection agency or the police. Many counsellors experience difficulty with reporting requirements for fear of violating the trust of a child, or creating mistrust with the child's parents. Such reporting to Children's Protective Services has saved the lives of many children, and brought help to families. Although children are still removed from their families and placed in foster homes when it is necessary for their protection, the emphasis has shifted to serving children in their own homes, and providing services to help the family overcome the situations which lead to abuse or neglect. Counsellors should be familiar with child abuse reporting laws in their own states. Typically counsellors and school personnel are required to report suspected abuse, and are granted immunity from liability because they are presumed to be acting in good faith. Many states also have criminal or civil penalties established for mandated professionals who fail to report.

Forms of Maltreatment

A common theme underlying most forms of maltreatment—physical abuse, neglect, or sexual abuse and exploitation—is that of emotional hurt. The child who is physically abused often suffers emotionally from inconsistent parenting and fear. The sexually abused child suffers from the lack of affection or supervision which leaves him/her vulnerable to the subtle advances of the perpetrator; and the neglected child becomes anxious or apathetic about a life in which basic needs aren't met. One general consequence of child maltreatment is developmental fixation or "freesing." The child who comes to the attention of the counselor due to difficulties in the classroom or poor social adjustment may very well be a maltreated child.

Neglect

Neglect accounts for more deaths than the physical abuse of children. In US, a national study of reported child maltreatment, only 4% experienced major physical injury, while 60% experienced a type of physical neglect. Neglect was associated with 56% of child deaths. All types of neglect are essentially a failure by the parents to provide something needed for the child's healthy growth and development. The concept of neglect includes the assumption that some harm must befall the child as a result of the parents' failure to provide.

Physical abuse

Physical abuse is usually defined as the intentional or nonaccidental inflicting of injury on a child by a caregiver. It manifests as bruises, welts, broken bones, burns, lacerations, or even death. It may occur through hitting, striking, beating, kicking, biting, slapping or other forms of violence directed at a child. Many, if not most, parents who abuse children have been reared in an environment in which some form of maltreatment occurred. Physical abuse appears in all socioeconomic classes, but is correlated with the stresses of poverty.

Sexual abuse and exploitation

Child sexual abuse is the adult (or older child) exploitation of the normal childhood development process, through the use of sexual activity. Examples of the types of sexual activity might include touching, kissing, fondling, manipulations of the genitals with the fingers, and actual sexual intercourse.

In examining patterns of sexual abuse and exploitation, it is important to keep in mind that the knowledge base is changing rapidly. While earlier belief was that sexual abuse perpetrators were almost always men, McCarty studied female perpetrators and found both accomplices who aided male perpetrators, and independent abusers, who had come from a background of bad childhoods, unhappy marriages and earlier sexual victimisation. Within the last decade it has been acknowledged that male children are also sexually victimised and are at great risk. It currently appears that female children are more likely to be sexually abused in an incestuous situation, while more male children are sexually abused outside the home.

Emotional abuse or neglect

Emotional neglect generally implies a consistent indifference to the child's needs and covers a range of behaviour, from the parent who never speaks to the child and doesn't remove the child from a crib, to the psychotic parent unable to acknowledge the reality of the child's world, or that the child actually exists. Emotional abuse, on the other hand, implies an active rejection or persecution of the child by the parent. Chronic verbal abuse erodes the child's self-esteem. The use of confinement or excessive punishment is also a form of emotional abuse. Emotional abuse or neglect is usually accompanied by other forms of maltreatment such as sexual abuse or physical abuse. Clearly, children who are being maltreated are not getting their developmental needs met.

Children who have been maltreated are usually unwilling or unable to reveal their situation to a counselor because of parental threats, or a feeling of loyalty to the family. While sensitive interviewing may help to unearth details of maltreatment, counsellors need to be aware of non-verbal ways in which the message of abuse may be communicated. The presence of one indicator alone does not necessarily mean that maltreatment has occurred. The counselor looks rather for configurations of indicators. If there are a number of indicators, the counselor has reason to suspect maltreatment, even if the child has not confided in the counselor.

Team approach

Counselling, in and of itself, cannot ensure the safety of a maltreated child. There will be many professionals involved in working with maltreated children. Typically, a Children's Protective Services worker may coordinate the intervention. Medical personnel will be involved. This may include a coordinating pediatrician who will follow the child's growth and development, several specialists and other health practitioners such as a physical therapist or public health nurse who has worked with the family. If the child must be removed from the home, the team may include a foster parent.

Educators and school personnel are also an important part of the team. They can help to monitor a child's day-to-day safety and progress, and can build programmes to help the child's self-esteem and enhance cognitive development. In dealing with situations where there is risk to a child, the counselor will find that a team approach accomplishes more for the child than the single intervention of offering counselling.

One of the primary purposes of counselling the maltreated child is to provide a safe place and safe relationship within which the child may experiment with new adaptations to a safer world, and in which the child's arrested development may become "unstuck." Counsellors cannot literally replace the requisite parental bonding which helps children to grow and develop, but have an opportunity to help the child develop a trusting relationship with an adult.

The key to understanding the maltreated child is to look at the developmental stage rather than the chronological age. The counselor will be able to identify adaptations which the child made to the maltreatment and teach the child more appropriate ways of interacting. Children often reveal in play the traumatic events of their earlier years. They may also show to the counselor maladaptive behaviour which puts them at risk of further maltreatment.

In the counselling relationship, working with maltreated children requires many techniques other than talking and listening. Using structured or unstructured play situations and artwork, music or clay provide a safe way for children to release tension and express themselves. Younger children do well with dolls and dollhouses to act out family issues for the counselor. Many maltreated children have not had normal play opportunities and benefit greatly from free play in the counselor's office. Using puppets, reading stories, or acting out role plays are ways in which abused children can try out new approaches to relationships.

Abused children also do well when counsellors work with them in groups. Younger children do well with developmental play groups, while older children and youth can benefit from activity groups as well as treatment-oriented groups. Group counselling can be especially useful with children and youth who have been sexually abused by reducing their feelings of shame and differentness and helping them to learn how to protect themselves.

Self-awareness of Counsellors

Counselling abused children is challenging in that it can arouse many complex feelings within the counselor. Anger with the child's parents, uneasiness over the child's acting out, or feelings of frustration and sadness are not uncommon for counsellors to face. Anxiety about protecting the children from further maltreatment may be a predominant theme for the counselor. It is important for counsellors working with the sensitive issues of maltreatment to seek consultation, supervision, or even treatment for themselves when they become overwhelmed with feelings. Recognising one's professional limitations can also be helpful. It is important to remember that counselling alone cannot protect children, and that any effective long-term intervention will require a concerted team approach and a community which cares enough to offer adequate resources for families. Children will be healed and protected as families are helped.

Identification Exercise

Career exploration typically involves investigating personal factors such as interests, aptitudes, values, and personal style, along with labour market considerations. This investigation can require considerable time, particularly if each factor is investigated separately through qualitative or standardised measures. Given the time limitations of most counselling situations, and the desire to be efficient and comprehensive, there is a growing need for new methods of career assessment. One such approach is the pattern identification exercise (PIE) which has been used effectively in both individual and group career counselling. PIE starts with past experiences and through an in-depth questioning process seeks to identify personal patterns which are of relevance in establishing career pathways.

A premise underlying PIE is that experiences which form the basis for career exploration can come from any aspect of life—the experiences of each person are unique and a detailed and careful examination of the experiences will reveal some common life patterns. To illustrate, a leisure activity such as playing tennis can be appreciated for its social elements, the physical activity, the opportunity for competition, or for some other reason. The way in which a person plays (the good times and the challenges) can reflect patterns about motivation, planning, attitude, and self-concept. Uncovering these patterns can reveal important personal insights which have direct relevance to career choice, job search, and job satisfaction.

The process of exploring experiences is undoubtedly as important as the questions used to stimulate discussion. The client is actively involved in the generation of information, the interpretation of meaning, and the application of new insights. A collaborative working relationship between counselor and client must be maintained throughout. The client is respected as the final authority in the identification of patterns. The counselor has an opportunity to provide input, but this is always done in a tentative manner after the client has had a full opportunity to identify patterns.

The number of experiences to be analysed varies depending on motivation level and the amount of time available. Typically, the analysis would not extend beyond two or three experiences. Each analysis has the potential to add new patterns, but there also will be considerable overlap. The counselor plays an important role in introducing the exercise, but the expectation is that the client will be able to work independently or with other people in a group to conduct further analyses. The client is learning a method of inquiry as well as identifying particular patterns.

PIE involves client and counselor in a defined exploration sequence. A considerable amount of information is generated prior to identifying patterns. It is often helpful for the counselor to take notes. If note taking is used, it should be discussed with the client who should have full access to the information.

The steps of inquiry which characterise PIE are:

1. Ask the client to think about some activity from leisure, education, or work which is particularly enjoyable. Once the topic has been identified, ask the client to think about a specific time when it was very enjoyable and a time when it was less so.

2. Have the client sequentially describe in detail the positive and negative experiences. Some open-ended questions can be asked at this point to facilitate a full description. Some of the issues to explore include the people involved, feelings, thoughts, challenges, successes, and motivations. Also, what are the dynamics that differentiate the positive and negative dynamics? Depending on the situation, it may be

helpful to question some of the contextual issues. Questions in this regard focus on how their interest developed over time and what they project for the future.

3. After a full discussion, have the client consider what types of patterns are suggested by the information. Give the client every opportunity to make connections and provide ongoing support and encouragement. Ask how each specific piece of information reflects something about the client, i.e., goals, values, aptitudes, personal style, interests.
4. At this point the counselor can provide some input. Counselor statements should be tentative and positively linked with client comments. While this can be an opportunity for reframing, it is important to not lose sight of the client's contribution.
5. Connecting the above information and analysis to specific career themes can now be addressed. As above, the client speaks first, followed by the counselor. The question here is how personal information relates to career choice and action planning.

The counselor serves as a guide for the analysis, but at some point clients should be encouraged to conduct their own independent inquiry (perhaps as a homework assignment).

In group counselling the counselor would start by demonstrating the inquiry process with a member of the group. Participants would be then paired off and instructed to follow the steps of analysis with one another. The counselor would serve as a consultant while the members discussed and analysed their experiences. After a designated period of time the group would come together for debriefing.

Bibliography

Agazarian,Y.M., *System-Centered Therapy for Groups*, Guilford Press, 1997.

Alonso, A., & Swiller, H.I., *Group Therapy in Clinical Practice*. American Psychiatric Press, Inc., 1992.

Barret, R. L., & Robinson, B. E., "Teenage fathers: A profile". *Personnel and Guidance Journal*, 1981.

Bernard, H. S. & MacKenzie, K.R. (eds.), *Basics of Group Psychotherapy*, Guilford Press, 1999.

Bion, W.R., *Experiences in Groups and other Papers*. N.Y.: Basic Books, 1959.

Childers, J. H., & Couch, R. D., "Myths about group counseling: Identifying and challenging misconceptions". "Journal for Specialists in Group Work," 1989.

Corey, M. & Corey,G., *Groups: Process & Practice* (5th ed.), Pacific Grove, CA: Brooks/Cole, 1996.

____________, "Groups: Process and practice" (4th ed.), *Pacific Grove*, CA: Brooks/Cole, 1992.

Dies, R.R. & MacKenzie, K.R., *Advances in Group Psychotherapy: Integrating Research and Practice*. N.Y.: International University Press, 1983

Fehr, S.S., *Introduction to Group Therapy: A Practical Guide*. N.Y.: Haworth Press, 1999.

Foulkes, S.H. & Anthony, E.J., *Group Psychotherapy: The Psychoanalytic Approach*. London: Penguin Books, 1965.

Gazda, G.M., *Group Counseling: A Developmental Approach* (4th ed.). Boston: Allyn & Bacon, 1989.

Gladding, S. T., "Effective group counseling." *Greensboro,* 1994.

Kaplan, H. & Sadock, B. (eds.), *Comprehensive Group Psychotherapy.* 3rd ed. Baltimore: Williams & Wilkins, 1993.

Lewin, K., "Resolving social conflicts: Selective papers on group dynamics." New York: Harper, 1948.

Lieberman, M.A., Yalom, I.D.& Miles, M.B., *Encounter Groups: First Facts.* N.Y.: Basic Books, 1973.

McClure, B. A., "The group mind: Generative and regressive groups." *Journal for Specialists in Group Work,* 1990.

Ormont, L.R., *The Group Therapy Experience.* N.Y: St. Martin's Press, 1992.

Parke, R. D., Power, T. G., & Fisher, T., "The adolescent father's impact on the mother and child". *Journal of Social Issues,* 1980.

Rogers, C.R., *On Encounter Groups.* N.Y.: Harper & Row, 1970.

Rutan, S.J. & Stone, N.W., *Psychodynamic Group Psychotherapy.* 3rd Ed. N.Y.: Guilford Press, 2000.

Tuckman, B. W., & Jensen, M. A., "Stages of small group development revisited". *Group and Organizational Studies,* 1977.

Index